Is Going to Uni Worth It?

Is Going to Uni Worth It?

A practical guide to choosing the right path for you

Michael Tefula

Is Going to Uni Worth It? A practical guide to choosing the right path for you

This first edition published in 2022 by Trotman Indigo Publishing Ltd,
21d Charles Street, Bath BA1 1HX

© Trotman Indigo Publishing Ltd 2022

Author: Michael Tefula

British Library Cataloguing in Publication Data

A catalogue record for this book is available from the British Library

ISBN: 978 1 91106 784 9

All rights reserved. No part of this publication may be reproduced, stored in a retrieval system or transmitted in any form or by any means, electronic and mechanical, photocopying, recording or otherwise without prior permission of Trotman Indigo.

The author's moral rights have been asserted.

Please note that all websites given in this book are subject to chang,e so you may find that some of these sites in time may be renamed, merge with other sites or disappear.

Printed and bound in Great Britain by Ashford Colour Press Ltd.

Contents

Preface	vii
Introduction	xi

Part One: Before You Decide

Chapter 1: The Art of Making Smart Choices	3
Chapter 2: Learning to Think Independently	17
Chapter 3: Getting to Know Your Underlying Dreams and Aspirations	31

Part Two: Possible Paths

Chapter 4: Going to University	45
Chapter 5: Doing an Apprenticeship	61
Chapter 6: Working Your Way Up	83
Chapter 7: Taking Time Out to Think	95

Part Three: How To Decide: The Five Key Factors

Chapter 8: Your Career Options	105
Chapter 9: Your Learning Preferences	117
Chapter 10: The Financial Costs	131
Chapter 11: The Future Financial Rewards	149
Chapter 12: Your Social Life	169

Part Four: Making Your Choice

Chapter 13: It's Decision Time	181
Chapter 14: Summing Up: Is Going to Uni Worth It – for You?	195

Acknowledgements	199
References	201

PREFACE

When you plan to write about something that you care about, it's easy to think you know how it's going to go. But every time I sit down to write something new, I'm always surprised by the unexpected turns that the process can take.

For this book, I *initially* set out to write a guide on how to choose between going to university or heading straight into work to train as an apprentice. And although it's possible to enter some industries straight from school, without a formal training programme, these two options – university and apprenticeships – were the *only* areas that I had intended to explore.

As I dug into these two paths, I expected to learn more about apprenticeships than university, to be honest, as I'm a university graduate myself. But I ended up being surprised by what I discovered about both options in equal measure – as well as about the options outside of these two paths. Ultimately, this led to me adding new material to the book in order to widen its scope – including two whole new chapters in the form of Chapter 6 about 'Working Your Way Up' in the world of work and Chapter 7 about 'Taking Time Out to Think' in the form of a 'gap year'.

An example of the kind of discoveries I made as I delved into my research is that, according to a 2020 report by the Institute of Fiscal Studies, one in five students in the UK are expected to be worse off financially by going to university. This means that an estimated 70,000 UK students every year would do better financially if they *didn't* go to university at all.

IS GOING TO UNI WORTH IT?

Other surprise discoveries were that construction apprenticeships – an area with a chronic skills shortage in the UK – can lead to individual annual earnings of more than £50,000; and a quality carpentry qualification is probably more likely to put you in the top 10% of earners in the UK than the average university degree. (Although, of course, this doesn't mean that you should ditch your own genuine interests in exchange for a construction qualification just for the sake of it.)

It was also surprising to learn that, even though university is increasingly expensive, it's adapting to what modern students need. For instance, some universities now offer accelerated degrees, where you graduate within two years, at a lower cost. Others are working ever more closely and creatively with businesses (for example, through work experience placements) to better prepare graduates for the world of work.

Although all these facts were interesting, it was conversations with young people themselves that inspired me the most, as it was they who opened my eyes to the fact that university and apprenticeships aren't the *only* viable choices when it comes to continuing education after school these days. People go about their journey in all sorts of different ways that can work out well for them – sometimes involving apprenticeships and/or university, and sometimes not.

Take Louis Curtis. At his school, apprenticeships were generally looked down on. 'Where I was from there was such a stigma about apprenticeships,' he recalls. 'But when I started to read about them it just started to seem like a bit of a no-brainer.'

Louis decided to embark on a Higher Apprenticeship (see the table on page 65 for more information on what this is and what it requires) and, after three years, received an engineering qualification from an established building materials business in

Leicester. But his ambition didn't stop there, as now that he had trained as an engineer, he knew that he could go further. 'I took a decision to reshape my career,' he explained.

Given that he'd spent time at the University of Derby for 'off-the-job' training and had done well enough on his assessments to consider a career in higher management, he took up the university's offer to jump straight onto a Master of Business Administration (MBA) degree.

In doing this, Louis effectively skipped the 'standard' three-year undergraduate route to doing a master's degree – a route that can lead to over £50,000 of student debt! Smart.

His *choice* of programme was smart too, as an MBA isn't just any master's degree – it's one that's known to be particularly useful for opening doors to positions of influence in business and management; one in four chief executive officers (CEOs) of the UK's largest businesses has an MBA.

It's usually quite tough to secure a place to do an MBA unless you have a good undergraduate degree and significant work experience. But Louis managed to do it, despite his background being different from the MBA 'norm', i.e. a recently qualified apprentice and also pretty young for an MBA candidate.

Louis' route was an exception in many ways, but his story – among the many others I have come across – reinforces the main takeaway of this book:

*You can have a bright future no matter which path you choose to take – as long as you make an effort to find what works best **for you**.*

INTRODUCTION

In some circles, going to university is a choice that's rarely questioned. Many in these circles believe that it's the surest path to a great career, and some see it as a rite of passage into adulthood and independence. But it's important to know that this view wasn't always the norm even in these circles. Universities were originally created to focus on academic scholarship and research, and only in relatively recent years has a degree been expected to prepare you for the actual world of work.

Today, the idea of going to university isn't just about fulfilling your academic curiosity. It's now also often considered the most obvious way to secure what is deemed a 'successful' future. But is university really the best decision for *you*, as an individual, based on what *you* view as 'successful'? As this book will show you, university is great for some people – but it doesn't mean that it's the right choice for everyone. *Your* task is to find out if it's the right choice for *you* – or if another path might suit you better.

My Choices

Like many college and sixth-form students of my time, I went to university. I had a strong curiosity about business, and without knowledge of any credible alternatives to university, I took an undergraduate degree in accounting and finance at the University of Birmingham.

I then trained as an accountant at the multinational company Deloitte on their graduate scheme (something you can now do via an apprenticeship route). After several years in the financial services industry, I enrolled at the University of Oxford for a master's degree.

With two degrees and an accounting qualification on my CV, hard work and a bit of luck soon led me to what was a dream job for me at the time – in the competitive field of venture capital, where I worked as a professional investor in technology companies for four years.

On reading my background, it would be easy to assume that I'm an advocate of the university route above others. After all, university served me well, and I have written three other books on how to do well academically and how to start a business after university. Yet, on doing the research for this book – which involved me speaking to lots of current and qualified apprentices, students, graduates, and people who took various other paths – I've realised that university simply isn't the best option for *everyone*. So why is this?

Is the Value of a Degree Shrinking?

University can be a soft landing into adulthood, independence and, eventually, the workplace. You typically spend three years learning as much about your chosen subject(s) as you do about yourself, and when you graduate, career doors can open more easily than they might otherwise have, depending on how well you do.

Around seven in ten graduates in the UK get a job within 15 months of graduation, and the majority of these end up in high-skill professions. In addition, graduates earn, on average, around

INTRODUCTION

£100,000 more over a lifetime compared to people who don't pursue any further qualifications after their A levels or equivalent.

Despite these benefits – which tend to hide the less positive reality of many individual cases and outcomes due to being based on *average* figures – the soaring costs of a university education have brought into question the value it delivers in the long term.

Consider how much a degree in the UK costs today compared to 2010. According to the Bank of England, tuition fees have had the largest price increase (over 150% in real terms) out of all the items they track. The chart below illustrates this rise against common items such as laptops, games, milk and beer, to the year 2018.

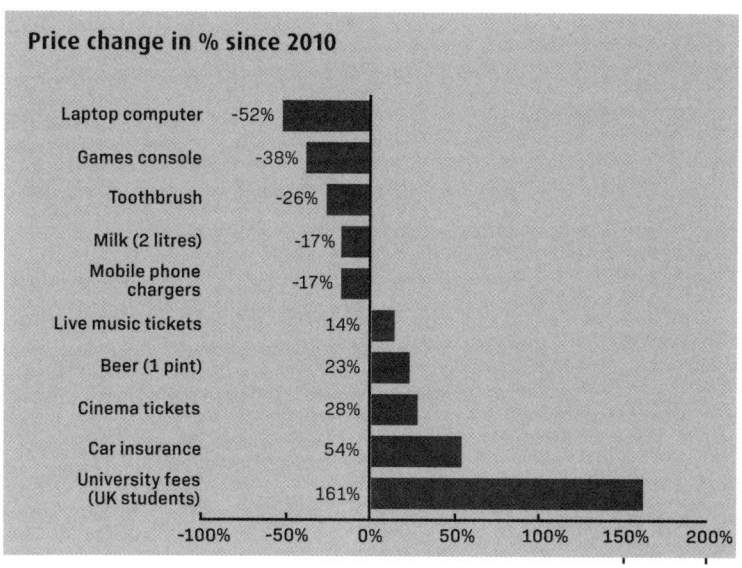

Research also suggests that the graduate advantage in the workplace is now shrinking. Data from the Higher Education Statistics Agency shows that, although older generations benefited plenty from their degree in financial terms, recent graduates are seeing lower returns on their investment. In addition, around half of today's UK graduates are said to feel unprepared for the world of work after university.

What About Apprenticeships?

It's considered by many that apprenticeships do a better job than university of preparing you for the *reality* of work. It's also a bonus that you get paid to train and, as you'll learn in Chapter 5, the majority of apprentices feel satisfied with their qualification. Furthermore, over 90% of apprentices remain in employment after their training.

Yet, the apprenticeship route is less known and less popular than university (fewer than one in ten 18-year-olds in the UK choose apprenticeships versus four in ten who choose a degree). Having said this, apprenticeships are now increasingly being recognised by big employers such as Google, Rolls-Royce, the BBC, and Marks and Spencer among others.

Apprenticeships aren't without their potential problems though. For example, you need to have a good idea about what career you might like to pursue before signing up for any particular course, and you need to be motivated to apply for lots of roles, since the best apprenticeships are often more competitive than getting into a top university.

It's now also possible to take a Degree Apprenticeship route. This is an apprenticeship that combines both academic learning in a university setting and well-paid practical training in the real world. This path typically takes three to six years to complete, involves full-time work and part-time study at a university, and allows you to avoid the perils of student debt!

INTRODUCTION

What Other Routes to the Workplace are There?

As briefly mentioned in the Preface, there are other routes besides going to university or taking an apprenticeship. Some students go straight into a job after school in order to 'work their way up' or train in a specific profession outside traditional paths (more on this in Chapter 6); while others take time out with a gap year to volunteer, work or explore other career options (more on this in Chapter 7). There's certainly no 'one path fits all' rule, which means that you have the luxury of choosing how to shape your own journey.

What Does All this Mean for *You*?

Given that you've picked up this book – with the title *Is Going To Uni Worth It?* – I'll make a guess that you're probably at least *considering* going to uni – you may even have already decided what you want to study and where.

Whatever your situation, now's your chance to give this option a bit more thought, making sure that you've properly assessed the range of paths available to the bright future that awaits you, rather than just making an almost 'automatic' decision, based on factors like what your mates are doing or what you feel you 'should' do. So, whether you bought this book for yourself, your parents or carers got you a copy, you were lent it by a friend, or whatever else, the hope is that it will offer you both support and insights during this exploration, helping you to be able to make a more informed and confident decision.

The chapters ahead will present you with a whole host of facts and figures to consider about the paths available, as well as sharing with you the direct experiences and insights of students who have gone to university, completed apprenticeships and also taken other routes into the world of work. Along the way, we'll dispel myths, clarify fuzzy areas like the mechanics of student loans, and generally flesh out the merits and weaknesses of the main options. By the end of the book, you'll be in a much better position to make a decision about what you want to do – one of the most important decisions that you'll make as a young person.

So if you're currently undecided about what to do next, don't worry – I'll be here, guiding you every step of the way. In Chapter 13 you'll even find a specific exercise that will help you to crystallise your decision.

On the other hand, if you're already set on going to university or if there's a specific degree that you know you would like to study, that's great, too. This book will help you to better understand the strengths and weaknesses of university. You can then aim to make up for those weaknesses if you want – for example, by getting work experience during the holidays, and/or alongside your degree if appropriate.

No matter which way you're leaning on the decision right now, know that by the end of this book you'll hopefully feel both more knowledgeable and more self-assured about your next steps.

About this Book

There are four core parts to this book and each one builds on the others. In Part One, **Before You Decide**, we will explore the art of empowered decision-making, with tips for minimising any anxiety you might be experiencing (Chapter 1); we will discuss how to deal with the influences and expectations of others yet still think independently (Chapter 2); and we will dig into the value of getting to know your underlying hopes and aspirations (Chapter 3) – all of which will help you to establish a positive mindset to make a decision that's right for *you*.

In Part Two, **Possible Paths**, we'll go through the nuances of the main paths open to you. We'll start with the two big ones: university (Chapter 4) and apprenticeships (Chapter 5). This is where most of the focus in the book will be since these are still the most established and popular routes – the ones whose resulting qualifications are most widely recognised by most employers and the ones that currently receive the most government and business support, with over two million participants a year between them in the UK alone (though university students make up the bulk of this number). However, in case these two choices don't resonate with you, we'll also consider the option, as mentioned earlier, of going directly into the workplace in order to 'work your way up' (Chapter 6) and the option of taking time out in the form of a gap year (Chapter 7).

In Part Three, **How to Decide: The Five Key Factors**, we will look at the five most fundamental elements when thinking about the path that's best for you. These factors – your career options (in Chapter 8), your learning preferences (in Chapter 9), the financial costs (in Chapter 10), the future financial rewards (in Chapter 11) and your social life (in Chapter 12) – all play a significant role in your decision, so understanding them is key.

In Part Four, **Making Your Choice**, you'll find an exercise to do (in Chapter 13) that will help you identify what could be the most suitable path for you. This requires a good understanding of the five factors from Part Three, so feel free to use the 'Recap' summaries in each chapter as needed. Lastly, in 'Summing Up'

(Chapter 14), you'll find (you guessed it!) a *summary* answer to the question that this book poses: 'Is going to university worth it?' Although, hopefully by that point, you'll already have an answer of your own, too.

Interwoven throughout the chapters, you'll also find **Insight** boxes that offer a mix of interesting facts and tips about education and training, and **Perspective** boxes that bring you the personal experiences of a range of graduates, apprentices and students who took alternative paths.

Taking Ownership of Your Decisions

No one person or book can prescribe exactly what you should do after school. Your decision will be personal and specific to your circumstances (although you can be sure that lots of people will have an opinion about it!). The decision truly is yours to make. And even if you might feel some pressure to meet other people's expectations, be they parents, grandparents, other carers, friends or teachers, it's really important not to lose sight that this is *your* future. So rather than have someone else decide for you or just go along with what you feel others want, it's important that you take ownership of the path you want to pursue.

This book aims to be your friendly (and knowledgeable) companion in that process. The hope is that by the end, you will have all the key information you need to answer the big question: Is going to university worth it – for *you*?

PART ONE

BEFORE YOU DECIDE

Making big choices is rarely easy – your GCSE and A level choices are just two examples of this. But why are some choices harder than others? How can you deal with parents', teachers' or anyone else's expectations about what you 'should' do after school? Have you thought about what *truly* motivates you and what kind of future you'd like? And is it possible to turn from feeling anxious or overwhelmed about such important choices into feelings of excitement and empowerment instead? This part of the book will help you think through all these important questions.

1
THE ART OF MAKING SMART CHOICES

Today, you have more options in almost every area of life than previous generations ever had. You can pick from millions of songs on Spotify, from just as many items from shops – both online and on the high street – and from hundreds of school-leaver career opportunities, including university courses, apprenticeship programmes or industry placements.

While more options can be good, too much of *anything* can become tricky. Think about the last time you went to a restaurant with an enormous menu, and compare it to a time when you went to a restaurant with a one-page menu – which situation caused less of a headache?

For most people, choosing becomes easier when options are less overwhelming, and, in some ways, that's the approach that this book takes as well. As already mentioned, the *main* focus will be on the choice between university and apprenticeships, rather than going into great detail about *every* education and training path that's possible. However, a number of other options will also be considered.

No matter how many options are being considered though, the choice is often hard, since direct comparisons aren't always possible. To help with this, we'll zoom out a bit in this chapter and take a big-picture view on how to approach hard choices in a smart way.

More specifically, this chapter will help you to build a mindset that reduces the worry and anxiety that can come with deciding what to do after school. And, as you become more comfortable with the decision-making process, you may well even be able to see it as an opportunity to uniquely express who you are and who you would like to be, rather than viewing it as any kind of burden or cause for stress.

What Makes Hard Choices So Hard?

Choosing what to do after school – especially if you decide for yourself, rather than follow what others expect of you – can be hard. But what is it that makes such choices so difficult?

According to the modern philosopher Ruth Chang, when you have an 'easy' choice, the best option is clear to you. In her popular YouTube video 'How to make hard choices', Chang expands on this point by highlighting that the difficulty of a choice is linked to how the available options relate to one another.

Let's consider a few everyday scenarios. It would be easy, for example, to choose the best football team when you're playing FIFA on PlayStation or Xbox, and have to pick between Brazil (one of the best football teams of all time) and Madagascar (currently ranked about 100 places below Brazil). The overall best option is obvious, even when you consider it against a variety of factors.

CHAPTER 1 THE ART OF MAKING SMART CHOICES

But if we take the example of choosing what style of shoe you'd like to buy – how could you know for certain what the best shoe is overall? There will be some factors that are easy to compare, such as size. But there will also be other factors that are harder to gauge, such as the satisfaction that a particular colour, material or style might give you. It may well be that when you look at the options available, one shoe will seem better in *some* ways while another will seem better in *other* ways.

And it's these more subjective factors that make any hard choice hard! After all, how could anyone ever *definitively* measure, or tell, which out of a range of shoes looks 'best' on someone? Different people will always have different opinions in different situations. For example, a particular style of shoe might seem perfect for your prom outfit, but would it also work with your day-to-day clothes? And you or your friends might love a particular shoe, but will your mother or grandmother, for example, love the same style?

Professor Chang has a possible solution to this problem. When thinking about hard choices, she suggests that you think about the options as being 'on a par' with one another (i.e. equal in value) and that you therefore try to appreciate them in *different* ways rather than torturing yourself with which one is overall 'better' than the other. Here's how she puts it:

> *When alternatives are on a par, it may matter very much which you choose, but one alternative isn't better than the other. Rather, the alternatives are in the same neighbourhood of value, in the same league of value, while at the same time being very different in kind of value.*

This very much applies to the choice of what to do after leaving school, as there's rarely one path that's the *absolute* best no matter what. Many different options are 'on a par' with one another and will therefore be valuable in different ways to different people. For instance, someone that chooses to train as a legal apprentice at a retail company would be looking for something quite different to someone who wants to study law at university.

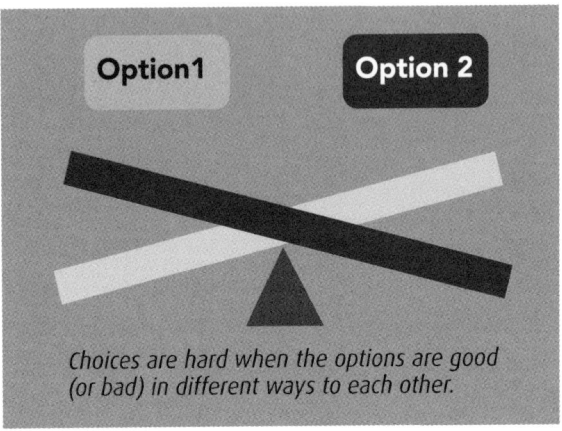

Choices are hard when the options are good (or bad) in different ways to each other.

The diagram above shows the double seesaw nature of hard choices – where each option has its own pros and cons for different individuals. Any choice where there is no definitive 'best' option is therefore **a hard choice!**

Finding empowerment in hard choices

Since hard choices don't have a one-size-fits-all answer, there is rarely much point in agonising over trying to find the scientifically 'best' option. In later chapters, we'll consider some key factors, such as financial costs and rewards, that can guide your choice in a somewhat objective fashion. However, factors like this cannot tell you the whole story. It is the qualitative factors – such as your personal preferences, passions and ambitions – that will complete the picture. And that's precisely the beauty of hard choices: knowing that you have the power in your very own hands to choose the thing that is right for *you*.

In addition, making hard choices is an opportunity to lean into, and grow, your own unique personality and character. We are, after all, defined by the hard choices that we make. Choice expert Ruth Chang advises that instead of going along with what others expect of us, choosing what we think other people will approve of, or making what seems like a traditionally 'safer' choice, it's always best to look inside and ask ourselves who we really want to be, and therefore what we want to do.

So, you might, for example, choose to enter the workplace directly to pursue a career in a field that you're passionate about; or you might choose to continue your studies through university to study a subject you love, with a view to maybe working in a related profession.

Whatever you choose, just remember that any hard choice presents an empowering opportunity for you to shape your destiny with a path that's truly yours.

Taking responsibility for your choices

Your choice of what to do after school could be the first really significant decision that you've had to make. But as life goes on, there will be many more such choices to make – from deciding where to rent or buy a house (figuring out where you want to live can be harder than it looks!) to changing careers (which many people do; I certainly have), among many others.

By taking responsibility now for what you want to do after school, you'll be training a muscle that will be invaluable time and time again as life goes on. And this training involves appreciating that, whatever you decide to do, it's *you* who has to live with the results of the decision that you make – not your parents, teachers, friends or anyone else.

The people around you will no doubt have opinions about what you should or shouldn't do – and it's always sensible, and potentially useful, to hear them out. However, ultimately, *they* aren't the ones who will have to live with the decision. It's *you* who will have to do the work that it takes to make a choice successful, and it's *you* who will have to overcome any potential challenges along the way.

For these reasons, deciding what to do after school is a fantastic opportunity to begin to own your own choices in life and embrace taking fuller responsibility for yourself.

Your choice *now* doesn't have to determine your whole life

Although it does, of course, matter what you decide to do after school, it's important to know that this decision doesn't have to determine the whole rest of your life. You have many more years of adventure and learning ahead of you, and there will be plenty more choices that steer the paths you take in life. And the good thing is that if you can calmly and confidently take control over this choice, you'll be able to do the same with other choices in the future.

For example, creative businesswoman and social media sensation Zoe Sugg (also known as Zoella) chose not to go to university after completing A levels in art, photography and textiles. She realised that staying close to her family would help her to manage her anxiety, plus she was uncertain about what she would study at university.

Instead, Zoe took an interior design apprenticeship at a local business and started a blog in her spare time. To her surprise, the blog quickly grew a substantial audience and ended up propelling her to the successful media career she has today – none of which she could have *predicted* when she chose what to do after her A levels, but none of which was hindered by these choices either!

CHAPTER 1 THE ART OF MAKING SMART CHOICES

Apprentice Perspective

Jamilah Simpson, Community Programmes Associate at Multiverse

Even if you do an apprenticeship in one area, it's still possible to then go on to work in another. Jamilah is proof of this, as she started off with a digital marketing apprenticeship at Google before branching into what she does at Multiverse now. Thinking back on things, she reflects:

> 'I was really indecisive... Even for my GCSEs and A levels, I picked subjects that I enjoyed as opposed to subjects that would lead to a specific career path, just because I didn't really know what I wanted to do. When I studied photography as one of my A levels, I discovered I really enjoyed the creative side of it and the tech elements to it. So I started researching industries that combine the two and came across digital marketing. It wasn't an area I had any experience in before my apprenticeship, but I just knew that I wanted to be in a creative industry.'

Jamilah's apprenticeship experience at Google helped her go on to secure a role at Multiverse, a fast-growth company that's working to change the future of work by making apprenticeships more widely accessible. Considering this now, she says:

> 'During my apprenticeship I was able to gain really valuable transferable skills that I still use in my role today. What I do now is more focussed on project management and a little bit of stakeholder management. So it's completely different to what I was doing my apprenticeship in, and I don't know if I'm going to continue this or move on to something completely new. But my ten-year plan is to have my own business.'

As you can see, Jamilah continues to keep an open mind about her development in the future.

Another example of someone who forged their own post-school route is Helen Barnes, who wrote about her journey in the *Daily Telegraph*. Helen initially worked as an executive assistant for a senior banker. But after doing this for many years, she felt that her career had plateaued and wanted to do something about it. Since Helen's work environment favoured certain qualifications and educational experience, she decided, at 28, that she would like to go to university, so she applied for a Management and Business degree at the University of York – as a mature student. This ended up being a great choice for her, as she went on to graduate with a first-class honours degree that helped her secure multiple job offers in her industry.

There are so many more examples of people who chose one route after school but who then went on to succeed in both related *and* unrelated ways, that it's clear the choice you make now doesn't have to determine everything else in your future.

And on top of this, it's important to remember that *whatever* path you end up choosing, there will *always* be invaluable things to learn along the way, such as problem-solving, critical thinking, communication skills and so much more – all of which can be used in many ways in life, including in many careers.

So long as you're thoughtful about the path that you take and approach it positively, you can have a happy, fulfilling career and life, whether you go to university or take another path.

Removing Anxiety from Choices

Whether you have a pretty good idea which way you're leaning when it comes to what to do next, or whether you're still completely on the fence about it, you might well be feeling a sense of nervousness and anxiety around the whole thing.

CHAPTER 1 THE ART OF MAKING SMART CHOICES

This could be coming from a number of places. You might, for example, have endured what feels like endless conversations starting, 'So what are you going to do next?', only adding to the feeling of pressure that you need to get this 'right'. You might be worried about making a choice that goes against the advice of people you care for and respect, whether parents, friends, teachers or whoever else – all of whom often *want* what's best for you but might not *know* what's right for you. You might be suffering from FOMO (fear of missing out), especially if the majority of your friends are choosing one particular route. And/or you might even be worrying about whether or not you're going to be able to get the best out of whatever route you choose to take.

So let's now have a look at some ways that you can dial down any such anxiety – in order to make your decision from a place of increased calm and confidence.

Research your options

Anxiety is worry about the unknown. So please know that it's only natural if you're feeling a little anxious about what you're going to do after school! I remember feeling really worried about how things would go after my A levels. In fact, not just then, but also after I left university and each time I changed jobs or had to make any other major choices in life.

Over the years, however, I've learned that you can drastically reduce worry when you invest time in properly researching your options. It's not that this is going to give you absolute certainty about the future; but what it will do is give you enough information to know how and why certain options are different, and how they could therefore play out in the future.

IS GOING TO UNI WORTH IT?

Think about the last time you had to decide something major – your GCSE or A level choices, for example – and how you made those decisions. Were your choices based purely on what subjects you enjoyed at the time, or were you thinking of the future? Have your plans changed since making those decisions, and if so, is that impacting your current process of deciding whether to go to university, do an apprenticeship or whatever else? Did anyone help you with your decisions? And, if you did have help from others, such as family, teachers or older students with experience of such decisions, did it prove useful? Would you listen to them again, or would you look elsewhere for advice next time you have a big choice to make?

Now imagine if you weren't allowed, or able, to get advice from anyone or anywhere else and had only your own limited experience to rely on. Wouldn't having to make your choice in a lonely vacuum like this make it all the more difficult to imagine the future impact of your choice? And wouldn't this contribute to more anxiety about the choice?

One of the first steps to help reduce any choice anxiety you may be experiencing is therefore to gather high-quality information that will help to guide your decision. This research can include seeking answers to questions such as:
- ▶ What options are available and accessible?
- ▶ What are the pros and cons of each path?
- ▶ How well have different options worked out for different types of people?

This book will help you get started on finding the answers to these questions, but feel free to complement it with your own research too.

CHAPTER 1 THE ART OF MAKING SMART CHOICES

Graduate Perspective

Francine Quaicoe, Sociology Graduate (now a Lecturer)

Francine wasn't sure at first about what she wanted to do for work in the future, but university felt like the necessary choice to her:

'I went to university because I thought it was the thing to do. It just so happens that I ended up using my degree in my career. I did have some ideas of what I might want to be, but I didn't know exactly what it was. For example, I knew that I wanted to work with young people, and that was it. At first, I wanted to be a youth worker, social worker, solicitor, probation officer, as well as a teacher. I was very confused.'

Ultimately, Francine chose to do a degree in Sociology, which meant a wide variety of careers opened up to her on graduation. She has gone on to become a lecturer, which she couldn't have done without a degree. So university paid off in Francine's case, even though she wasn't entirely sure what she would do with her degree when she embarked on it. Today, Francine advises students to be thoughtful about their choices:

'I don't always recommend university. I ask students what they want to be in the future. And if they tell me a nurse or a doctor, I ask them to research how to become a doctor or how to become a nurse, so that they don't go into it blindly. My advice is to research what you want to do, why you want to do it and how to get there.'

One thing to remember about this process though: you want to gather enough information to help firm up what you would like to do, but not so much that the information overwhelms you. Knowing a wide range of facts and opinions about a choice will reduce worry, but not if you allow yourself to fall down a rabbit hole of endless research. It's therefore about finding balance in your approach.

Take positive action early

Often, you can only understand a choice more fully when you decide to lean in to one of the options. It's a bit like a jigsaw puzzle: only once you make an initial decision and just get on with things in a particular area will the overall picture start to become clearer. The guidance in this book will reveal some pieces of the puzzle to you but other parts will only be revealed when you take some definitive action.

As other parts of the puzzle then become clear – such as the practical realities of your chosen path and a deeper knowledge of yourself (this one takes time) – you can always still look at other alternatives if you realise that the choice you've made isn't quite right for you. For example, if you decide by the end of this book that you would like to pursue a specific apprenticeship, but you later discover things about it that aren't a good fit for you, there's absolutely nothing stopping you from simply changing your mind and pursuing a different path, whether that's another apprenticeship, a university route or something else.

The key message here is this: be confident in pursuing whatever route feels right to you, as you'll always learn something valuable from the process of *doing*. Taking positive action, whatever direction it is in, will ultimately always get you closer to achieving your full potential, even if there may be a few detours along the way.

'Good enough' beats 'perfect'

There are many ways to live life. But two opposing approaches when it comes to decision-making are: constantly searching for the 'perfect' choice versus always trying to make a 'good' choice.

With the first approach, you spend ages thinking about every option that you have in an attempt to always find the 'best' answer. Psychologists call people who take this path 'maximisers' – they seek to maximise every situation by finding what is perfect, even though, in reality, that perfect thing may not exist.

With the second approach, you set some realistic criteria and when you find something that meets them, you commit to that option as 'good enough', eliminating any need to then ruminate on whether you could have found something 'better.' Psychologists call these people 'satisficers' – they find satisfaction in what they identify as 'good enough', rather than endlessly chasing perfection.

Which group do you think is happier? The one that seeks perfection (and *perhaps* achieves it at times) or the one that aims for 'good enough' (who almost always achieve it)?

Psychologists have found that 'satisficers' (who are okay with 'good enough') tend to be happier than 'maximisers' (who seek the absolute best). Possible reasons for this include the drawn-out agony of searching for the very best in everything, the constant self-questioning about whether a longer search could have resulted in something better and the pressure of high expectations that are hard to live up to.

This tells us something useful about how it's usually best to approach big decisions, like whether to go to university or pursue another route – mainly that you're more likely to be satisfied by making what you feel is a 'good' choice than trying to make the 'perfect' one (which may not even exist!).

Having said that, it's important, of course, to know that if a choice ends up *really* not feeling right for you, or 'good enough', there's no harm in using your newly acquired knowledge to revise your decision. But as a first rule, aiming for 'good enough' is a straightforward route that's likely to involve a lot less anxiety than aiming for 'perfection'.

Chapter Recap

▶ Deciding what to do after school can be a hard choice as there's no definitive 'right' thing to do. Some options will be good in some ways; other options good in others.

▶ Since there's no one right course of action, try to embrace the opportunity to choose something that's a unique expression of who you are and who you want to be.

▶ Remember, your choice – whether you go to university, take up an apprenticeship or pursue something else – doesn't have to seal your fate forever; you can always change track and try other things as you learn more about yourself, and life.

▶ There's no such thing as a perfect choice, so aim to simply make a 'good' choice and be contented with this. This approach will bring you more satisfaction – and less worry.

2
LEARNING TO THINK INDEPENDENTLY

Deciding whether to go to university or not is _your_ decision, which means that it requires strong, independent thinking. However, it's natural to care to a certain extent what other people think of you. So in order to choose what really feels right for you, you may well need a good dose of bravery – to be bold enough to go against the grain if required.

That isn't to say that caring what other people think or expect of us is always bad. For example, have you ever felt like you disappointed someone you respect and then been motivated to do better in the future as a result? In cases like these, caring what others think (especially people who understand you and care about your future) can drive us to realise our full potential.

However, you have to be careful not to care so much that you lose your sense of agency. In other words, if everything you do is done out of a need to please parents, teachers, family, friends and other people in general, you might end up living the life that someone _else_ wants, rather than the life that _you_ want!

Thankfully, it's possible to make independent decisions without turning into an argumentative pain in the neck! You just need to strike a balance between being aware of external influence, while also taking a critical approach to your decision-making. This chapter will help you with this balancing act.

In the sections that follow, we'll look at the most common influences and expectations about what you should do after school. We'll briefly look at what's wrong with the assumptions that many people make about the most common choice – university. And we'll explore how to manage expectations and influences, as well as how to think more critically about whether university is the best choice for you, or not.

Alternative Perspective

Sven Aars-Rynning, Business Executive

People sometimes follow their parents' educational journey but that wasn't the case for Norwegian-born Sven Aars-Rynning. Although his father went to university and worked as a diplomat and lawyer, Sven took a different path. He decided not to get a degree and instead set out to build Norway's largest staircase cleaning company (it services 7,500 staircases a month). Sven's determination outside of school paid off, when, years later, he was able to sell his company successfully. Today, he advises young people to be bold and independent in their thinking:

> 'When you're growing up, your parents and everybody else always have expectations for you in many ways. But I believe the most important thing to do is to remove all the expectations. For example, I went to university for one year and I understood very fast that many people who went there should never have been there. They were there because their parents wanted them to be economists or whatever. But I believe that people should do what they really want to do, instead of following what their parents want them to do or what their friends want them to do. If you really want to do something, do it. Because a lot of people, in my opinion, waste a lot of time when they don't find their own way.'

CHAPTER 2 LEARNING TO THINK INDEPENDENTLY

Navigating Influences and Expectations

Your thoughts about whether or not to go to university may already have been influenced by what you've heard from your parents, teachers, family, friends and so on – both in terms of their *own* experiences and insights, and also in terms of their expectations of *you* – that is, the choice that these people think you 'should' make.

Even though these influences and expectations are often well-meaning, it's important to consider them critically, as *wanting* the best for someone isn't the same as *knowing* what's best for someone. So let's look at a few examples before we consider how you can nurture more independent thought in your decision-making.

Do parents always know best?

Parents and other carers often have the most influence on what route you take after school – especially as they may well be continuing to support you financially as you move into this next stage of your life. And there are usually a lot of positive sides to their influence. For example, your parents have more life experience than you, they know you well (even if you don't share everything with them!), and their interest in your choices tends to come from a place of love. It therefore makes sense to take their thoughts and opinion into consideration. However, it's important to remember that they are human too, so don't always get things right! Plus, their ideas of – and expectations around – what you should do might not entirely fit with your own interests and aspirations. Sometimes *their* hopes and expectations of you might even be more based on what they themselves enjoyed and found fulfilling, or what they *wish* they had done (or had the chance to do) when they were your age. As such, their desires and expectations could, at times, be misguided despite being well-intentioned!

Take the example of a family where it's tradition for everyone to go to university – no questions asked. In a case like this, the parents may encourage their child to take the university route because they believe that if it worked for them, it will work for their child too. But how could anyone be certain of this, given that their child is a whole different person, with potentially different interests, skills and aspirations? And let's not forget just how many more options for further education and training there are these days.

In other instances, if other members of your family *haven't* been to university, it is likely to impact their thoughts about you going in a different way. It may mean, for example, that they think there's no need for you to go, as *they've* done fine without it. Or it may mean that they're particularly keen on the idea of you having the opportunity to go, especially if they believe a degree will provide better prospects than what *they* had at a similar age. But again, how could they be sure of this without considering whether you, *personally*, might thrive more if you pursued other options?

Without knowing the full extent of the options available these days or considering what's *specific* about your needs, many parents remain in the dark about what's possible beyond the traditional route(s). This means that some parents risk putting undue pressure on their son or daughter to make a choice that feels familiar and 'safe', even if another path might be better.

On the whole, parents and other carers do want what's best for you though. So it's good to listen to any guidance and encouragement that they offer and to discuss things calmly with them, including asking them questions about *why* they might be suggesting certain things – so that you can have a healthy dialogue about it and really understand where they're coming from. Doing this will

CHAPTER 2 LEARNING TO THINK INDEPENDENTLY

> **Apprentice Perspective**
>
> ### Grace Morris, Higher Level Apprentice in Retail Management (now a Deputy Store Manager at Marks and Spencer)
>
> Grace comes from an academic family but since she knew that the career that she wanted in retail didn't need a degree, she opted for another suitable training path that avoided student debt. Her family knew her motivations well and, thankfully, they were all fully onboard with her decision. She explained:
>
>> 'Both of my parents went to the Royal Veterinary College, London, and went on to be vets. My grandparents include a doctor, an author, a counsellor and a scientist, so I am the first in about three generations not to go to university. My family have been encouraging with my career path because of my motivation and the make-up of the apprenticeship I was doing. By doing a Higher Apprenticeship in Retail Management, not only am I setting myself up to gain a qualification in higher education, but I also have the opportunity to be taught the skills to become a Store/Deputy Manager of Marks and Spencer stores in Central London, one of the most high-profile regions in the business and a position that can stem growth without the need for further higher education.'
>
> Grace did indeed go on to become a Deputy Store Manager at Marks and Spencer.

allow you to respectfully take on board what they say but frame it within the context of what you're discovering through your independent research.

Are teachers too pro-university?

You will have spent many hours under the guidance of teachers at school, so their influence is significant. Especially the ones that you like and respect!

Since teachers are specialists in education and learning, it's worth listening to them when thinking about your future. However, be mindful that the expectations of teachers on what you should or shouldn't do after school can (just like those of parents and other carers) be biased.

For example, a survey in 2018 found that only 21% of teachers in the UK would recommend apprenticeships to high-performing students. It is also reported that many teachers think university is superior (bear in mind that almost all teachers have a university degree themselves). It's therefore no big surprise that university is often the first choice of teachers for their students. Unfortunately, this particular survey also found that over a third of pro-university teachers lacked enough information and knowledge about alternative routes to offer a balanced view.

So, while most teachers aren't without good intentions and will want what's best for your future, it's important to remember that, just like your parents, they might not know enough about apprenticeships and other paths to be able to offer you sound advice on them.

Friends – is FOMO worth stressing over?

'You are the average of the five people you spend most time with,' said the American motivational speaker Jim Rohn. Now obviously this isn't entirely true (and if you're the maverick in your friendship group, you'll know this all too well). But the quote has some truth to it.

The more time we spend with our friends, the more we become like them. Over time, their influence can easily grow to be stronger than that of our parents, carers or teachers. Just think about the music you listen to, the clothes you wear, the books you read or the hobbies you have. One way or another, you've probably been influenced to some degree by your friends in a lot of these choices.

It's no wonder then that if all your friends happen to be deciding to take a specific path after school, you might feel inclined to do the same thing. You would have to battle against some serious FOMO if you were to go against the popular choice!

Be wary of this though. We are all different, so it's important to take a step back from your circle of friends to work out what is *really* the most promising choice for you. There's no denying that it could be great fun to embark on the same journey as all your friends – whether that's going to university or elsewhere. But it's worth considering that more often than not, the initial choice is where the similarity of the journey ends. Eventually, your school friends are likely to end up with different careers and maybe in different cities. FOMO might seem urgent now, but, in the long term, everyone ends up having their own unique journey.

Are the expected 'norms' about education changing?

You might still come across some people these days who have an unconscious (or perhaps even overt) expectation that 'educated' people have degrees. Some employers might also think that the 'university experience' (which is likely just to be what *their* experience of university was) makes someone more capable. But this type of 'educationism' – i.e. a bias that favours people with traditional academic backgrounds – mistakenly assumes that a degree itself is what makes you capable. What actually matters is the underlying mindset – of hard work, dedication etc – that allows you to achieve your potential, regardless of whether this process involves a degree, an apprenticeship or any other form of training.

> **Insight**
>
> **Differing education and training trends**
>
> Did you know that societal norms about education and training are different based on time and place? Here are two brief examples of this phenomenon.
>
> **Time differences**: In recent years, around half of young people in the UK go to university annually but only 30% did so in the early 1990s and just 5-10% did so in the 1960s. For previous generations, university simply wasn't the norm; it only became the dominant path after significant government investment. And this dominance is now starting to decline, as apprenticeships receive both more funding and recognition nationally.
>
> **Geographical differences**: While university may have become the most established educational path in the UK over recent years, *apprenticeships* are a national treasure in Germany. Around half of young people take part in the country's dual vocational and educational training programmes (called 'VET'), and they get to choose from over 300 recognised professional trades. The programmes work so well that they are quoted as one of the reasons why Germany has had the lowest youth unemployment rate in Europe for many years.

Fortunately, the rise of apprenticeships, online education and other personal development pathways makes it possible for you to achieve your potential in multiple ways these days. So rather than rely on what you feel is expected of you, or what many people say is 'best' overall, it's good to rely instead on what you feel best matches your personal profile and needs – whether that's a university degree or otherwise.

CHAPTER 2   LEARNING TO THINK INDEPENDENTLY

Are people's perceptions about university outdated?

Although some parents, teachers and others can, at times, show a bias towards university being the surest path to a good career after school, this assumption doesn't match up to modern reality. For example, research in 2018 found that one in four graduates in England and Northern Ireland were 'overeducated' (i.e. in jobs that didn't require a degree), yet they weren't necessarily over-*skilled*. In fact, according to the economic research group the OECD (the Organisation for Economic Co-operation and Development), around one in ten people in England and Northern Ireland actually leave university without the maths, reading and writing skills that would be expected of graduates in a workplace.

Of course, university has many benefits, but as later chapters will reveal, some of these are not enjoyed equally by all graduates. For instance, someone with a first-class degree from a top university in a traditional subject like Engineering could benefit massively from their degree (certainly in financial and career terms), whereas a graduate with a low grade in a less traditional subject from a relatively unknown university, on the other hand, might not fare so well.

So just how many people end up not financially benefiting from their university education? As mentioned earlier, the Institute for Fiscal Studies estimated in 2020 that one in five students in the UK would become financially worse off by going to university. That's a whopping 20% of young people who would be financially better off if they didn't go to university!

All in all then, it seems that the idea that some people hold of university being the 'best' educational path after school is clearly open to debate these days. After all, not all degrees and not all universities are created equal. It's much more complex than that. And even if they were, university isn't a good fit for everyone.

> ## Apprentice Perspective
>
> ### Haider Ali, Higher Level Apprentice in Management Accounting at Rolls-Royce
>
> Sometimes it's hard to get the support of your family if you try to do something different from what they consider the 'norm', or what they expect from you. So it's worth looking into whether you might have someone in your circle of family and friends who has relevant knowledge or experience and would be willing to provide you with emotional support, as well as potentially helping you win over your family. High-achieving A level student Haider Ali felt lucky to get this kind of help from his uncle when he decided to opt for an apprenticeship over a degree:
>
>> 'I come from a South Asian background and a degree is seen as the pinnacle of educational attainment. It's like, if you've got a degree, that's it – you've made it. You're clever, and you're guaranteed a job – "You've done the family proud" kind of thing! But it was my uncle, who works in finance in London and had taken the traditional university route, who reassured me that I wasn't crazy for wanting to take the apprenticeship route. He said that it was actually amazing. And he facilitated the discussion with my parents to basically say that, as someone who went to university, if he had had this opportunity at my age, he would have done it. And I think that's what made my parents realise that actually, no, this is something that's serious. It's not just something I want to do for the sake of it. There's actual value here. It's just that it's a new opportunity that a lot of people haven't quite clocked on to.'

Some people simply wouldn't thrive on the kinds of courses and the teaching approaches on offer there. Other people maybe *would* thrive in that environment, but only if they happen to find the specific place and the specific degree that's a fit for *them*.

So, when faced with the influence that other people will have on your decision, and the expectations they might have of you, it pays to take a *critical* approach. This means questioning the notion that many people still have of university being a supposedly failsafe option over anything else. In the next section, we'll look at the practical aspect of how you can develop this critical ability.

How to Make More Independent Decisions

Step 1: Be conscious and critical of external pressures

When making any decision, it's helpful to be aware of external influences acting on you. This includes other people's opinions and their expectations about your choices.

As we learnt earlier, influences and expectations aren't necessarily bad things; they can sometimes nudge you in the right direction. But it's useful to be conscious of them so that you can assess for yourself whether or not they have merit.

For example, if you feel pressure from your parents about taking a certain path, try not to see it as a negative. Their *intentions* will be good – they want you to do well. They just might not fully appreciate all the options available to you, or what's specifically right for you as an individual. See if you can use the content of this book as a starting point for discussion with them – so that they can learn and explore what routes are possible *alongside* you.

You can also take this approach with other sources of influence and expectation. For instance, if you feel pressure from your school about a particular path, feel free to ask the teachers concerned what they know about alternatives paths in comparison to their recommended one – in order to get a sense of their breadth of knowledge. They might only be suggesting what they know rather than what you need!

Step 2: Give less weight to what others think

This is easier said than done. But to be a more independent thinker – and therefore be more likely to take a path that's a good fit for you – you shouldn't care (too much) about what other people think of your decisions. Here's why:

▶ **You can't please everyone.** No matter what you do, there will always be people who approve of your choices and people who don't. Attempting to please everyone in life is therefore generally a miserable pursuit.

▶ **You're the one that has to live with your decisions.** Why care so much about what others think when they won't be in your shoes living out your decision? If you blindly follow the paths that others expect, you may end up living someone else's life. And if the paths don't work out, you might resent the people who led you there.

▶ **You're the only you.** Other people will suggest decisions that worked for them but those same choices won't necessarily work for you. You're an individual, so your situation has to be considered on its own merits.

Step 3: Develop your critical thinking skills

The previous steps were about setting aside undue influence and pressure, but when thinking about big decisions, you also have to make sure that you think critically. In other words, be prepared to question things more, and ask others what evidence they have to back up their claims.

You're likely to have already gained experience of critical thinking skills in the course of your A level studies, but here are some pointers that work reliably:

▶ **Ask why.** This is about going deeper on an issue. So, for example, if someone advises you to take a particular route, be sure to ask them *why* they think it's better, looking for specifics rather than just general comments. If you can't get an explanation for the 'why', try to do some research of your own to see if you can gain a better understanding.

▶ **Look for counter-arguments.** It's natural to look for things that confirm thoughts that we have already had, or decisions that we have already made. But to get the full picture, you have to also look for things that challenge your 'normal' thinking. Each path you consider will have pros and cons; it's just easier to miss the cons if you're already convinced about the superiority of a particular option, and also to miss the pros if you're already convinced about the inferiority of an alternative.

▶ **Use more than one source.** It's important not to rely on just one source – whether that's a person, book, website or whatever else – when weighing up your options. If you do rely on just one source, it's easy to miss crucial information. As well as reading this book, it would therefore be smart to consult your family, your teachers and anyone else you know who might be able to shed light on your options, as well as to do online research in areas that you're interested in. All of these approaches *combined* will better arm you with the information you need to make a good choice.

Chapter Recap

▶ We are influenced by a wide range of people and factors when making decisions – from the opinions and expectations of parents, other family members, teachers and friends to commentaries from wider society.

▶ Sometimes influences and expectations can be good at nudging us in the right direction, especially if they come from people who know us well and want what's best for us.

▶ Influences and expectations can, however, also be misguided and out-of-date, so be ready to set them aside if you wish to think more independently and critically.

▶ The university path is one that people sometimes assume to be the 'best' path. Yet, there are graduates who don't get the skills they need from their degrees. In addition, one in five students in the UK are expected to be worse off financially by going to university.

▶ Your decision-making process will benefit from independent, critical thinking. You can achieve this by asking people *why* they are making certain recommendations, looking for counter-arguments to your usual ways of thinking, and using multiple sources of information for your research.

3
GETTING TO KNOW YOUR UNDERLYING DREAMS AND ASPIRATIONS

'What do you want to be when you grow up?' is a question you might have been on the receiving end of since you were old enough to answer. Many adults love asking it, even though the question itself – which is mostly about what kind of job you'd like to do rather than what kind of life you'd like to live – can raise mixed emotions.

There are, no doubt, a few lucky people who can answer this question with ease – people who have known from a young age what career they would like to pursue, which makes it easier for them to choose what to do after school. But for the majority of people (and maybe this includes you?), the answer to the question isn't clear, so asking it raises a lot of doubt.

In either case, this career question misses something significant. It doesn't set you up to think about the *broader* aspirations that motivate career ideas – things like the kind of life you'd like to live and the *underlying* aspects of a job that you're drawn to.

Consider the examples of an aspiring journalist or pilot. It's possible that someone who wishes to be a journalist actually *aspires* to be in any well-respected job where they get to inform the public about issues that affect their lives. Likewise, someone who wants to be a pilot may *aspire* to work in any area where they live a life of travel, but with hands-on technical service work. Such aspirations contain valuable insights into your personal preferences and potential that can lead to a whole host of career options beyond the obvious. With some imagination and research, you too can plan for a future that has several routes to success and satisfaction.

Insight

Examples of how underlying aspirations can impact educational choices

	Various students	
	Student 1	
Underlying Aspirations	• Wants to help people in need • Seeking a respected profession • Enjoys working in the community	
Potential Training Path	**University career route:** Social Work Degree **Apprentice career route:** Public Health Practitioner Degree Apprenticeship	

CHAPTER 3 GETTING TO KNOW YOUR UNDERLYING DREAMS AND ASPIRATIONS

This is what we'll cover in this chapter. We'll start by asking why it's good to be mindful of aspirations when thinking about your dream job(s). We'll then consider specific aspirations that can set you up for a more hopeful future, whatever educational path you choose to pursue.

Why Thinking About Aspirations Matters

Aspirations are the general hopes you have for your future. Sometimes they are clear and vivid – for example, you may be drawn to a specific career, such as medicine or architecture,

Student 2	Student 3
• Wants to travel lots	• Not sure about aspirations
• Seeking technical challenges	• Seeking a secure career
• Enjoys different cultures and experiences	• Enjoys working with numbers
University career route: International Relations Degree	**University career route:** Maths Degree
Apprentice career route: Broadcast Operator Apprenticeship	**Apprentice career route:** Actuarial Technician Apprenticeship

after school. At other times they can be fuzzy but unconsciously motivating – for example, you might not know exactly what you want to do after school, but you might know that you want to work in a creative role to nourish a passion for the arts; in healthcare to fulfil a desire to care for others; or in the financial industry to exercise your passion for numbers.

To get to know your own aspirations better, ask yourself questions like 'What kind of life do I want?', 'Who are my role models?' and 'What specific things about these people might I aspire to?' Getting to know your innermost hopes and desires in this way can benefit you in two main practical ways...

First, if you consider your deeper aspirations – not just the specific job that you dream of for instance, but the underlying wishes – you may learn that there are actually many ways those aspirations can be met, irrespective of what educational route you take.

Take someone who wants to be a counsellor. If they reflect on the deeper reasons why that career is appealing to them, they might realise that it's because they find it rewarding to give advice to people. If that's the case, could there be other careers and pathways that fulfil this interest? Certainly. They could, for example, train as a strategy consultant, a writer (such as a newspaper columnist), a teacher or a lawyer – all careers where you offer useful advice.

The second reason that thinking about aspirations is important is that it's an opportunity to reflect on whether certain broader goals are definitely worth prioritising in the first place. This is because while some aspirations are tempting, they don't always deliver what they promise. In fact, if you pursue them single-mindedly you could veer off-course from your true calling.

One example of this is when people choose a specific career because they aspire to be rich. Sometimes this works out, if they actually enjoy the chosen career as well. But in other cases, people can look back on their decision with regret because of how much time they spent doing something they didn't enjoy, all just to make more money.

> ## Graduate Perspective
>
> ### Dr Laura Gill, Medicine graduate
>
> Laura had fleetingly considered the idea of being a doctor early on, but it wasn't until she got to choosing her A levels that she gave the decision deeper thought. Reflecting back on her choice – now that she's a doctor who loves what she does – Laura remembers how she got to where she is today:
>
> > 'Medicine appealed because I enjoyed the analytical nature of science but knew I wanted a job involving people. It's a cliché, but the idea of a career helping other people seemed fulfilling. I was also keen to travel, and an episode of the medical drama *ER*, where a character works with Doctors without Borders, put the idea of working as a doctor overseas into my head! I managed to do some work experience in a hospital but, honestly, I think it's hard to know which career is going to work for you while you're still at school. I wasn't 100% sure being a doctor was the right fit for me when I applied, or even when I started university, but I knew that I would always wonder if I didn't at least give it a shot.
> >
> > 'Now, I'm so glad I made that decision, and think it was the right choice. However, if I'd realised medicine wasn't for me, I don't think my time at university would have been wasted. A medical degree is generally held in high regard – employers see it as a marker of academic ability and aptitude for hard work. So, although changing my mind about becoming a doctor wouldn't have been ideal, I felt secure that my degree would still hold value even if I ended up working in a different field. I also chose a course where you got a BSc halfway through your medical degree – something that is increasingly common. I felt that would mean I could pursue another career at that point but still have a degree behind me if I realised being a doctor wasn't for me.'

There's nothing wrong, of course, with a desire for financial security. We all need it. But too much focus on this one aspiration can restrict us from choices that are better for us in the long term. Taking into account other aspirations, such as 'making a difference' (as cheesy as this might sound) may well lead to a career that you'll find more meaningful and fulfilling. So let's now explore this in a bit more detail.

Distracting Aspirations

Money, money, money

Having a job with a high salary can afford a life with many advantages. However, making choices based solely on the aspiration to make lots of money isn't always the best idea.

There are plenty of cautionary tales warning against the pursuit of gold above all else, from King Midas in Greek mythology (whose 'golden touch' ends up causing him problems by turning the things he loves the most – including his daughter – into lifeless gold) to the Cave of Wonders in the tale of Aladdin (which collapses when the forbidden treasure is touched). Indeed, there may be more truth in such tales than we often like to admit.

Although research has shown time and again that having a lot of money doesn't impact our happiness as much as we think, and it's generally well known that money doesn't buy lasting happiness, this pearl of wisdom doesn't always fully sink in when we think about wealth.

The reality about money is this: so long as we make enough of it to satisfy our basic needs, such as food, shelter, health and wellbeing, *more* wealth doesn't make us *massively* happier. In fact, it has been proven that as we make more money, it generally only makes us a tiny bit happier than the last increase in wealth.

So why is this? Here are a few of the reasons:

▶ **You get used to it.** Remember those new shoes you were dying to get or that latest gadget? How quickly did the novelty wear off after you got the goods? In other words, how soon does something you buy become just another item in your collection? We are creatures of habit, so after we get everything that money can buy, it doesn't take long to return to whatever our 'usual' state of happiness is.

▶ **You give up something else.** If you spend a lot of time and energy trying to 'get rich', you will more often than not end up with less time for other important things in life, such as friends and family. Putting money ahead of everything else might also mean you choose work that doesn't fulfil your true interests.

▶ **The goalposts keep on moving.** Psychologists have found that people tend to be a little happier if they see themselves as richer and/or of higher status than other people. However, there will always be wealthier and higher status people wherever you go, so the wealth and status game becomes an endless cycle, with ever-moving goalposts that can leave you feeling constantly dissatisfied. It's therefore better to not play that game at all!

To be clear here, money is in no way a bad thing! It can give you more freedom and ease in life, and it's important to secure your financial future; in fact, we'll look at the financial rewards of university and apprenticeships in Chapter 11. Just remember that once you have enough wealth to look after yourself and those you care about, more money won't necessarily make you all that much happier.

Fame and admiration

Lurking alongside the common desire for wealth is often the desire for fame and recognition. Fame can certainly bring with it a lot of perks, such as fast-track access to all sorts of people who can help your career – as well as freebies of course. Being famous can also make you feel admired and, as such, feel more significant to other people – something that we all crave.

However, fame also comes with a price, including things like loss of privacy, media intrusion, the judgement of strangers, not knowing if new friends are genuine or just hangers-on, and the fickle nature of the public's tastes.

Although tempting then, fame can come with its fair share of problems, which means it's not an ideal aspiration to prioritise as you think about what you'd like to do after school or for your dream career. That said, if you do happen to become famous, be sure to cash in on all the freebies!

Worthwhile Aspirations

Although we've just looked at how the pursuit of money and fame can distract us from making decisions that are true to ourselves, we can't completely ignore the personal needs from which the desire for these things stem. Our desire for more money, for example, is at least partially based on us wanting to be able to provide, without worry, for ourselves and our loved ones (as well as being able to treat ourselves every now and then). Meanwhile, our desire for fame often comes from us wanting to feel recognised and 'significant', with access to as many opportunities in life as possible.

CHAPTER 3 GETTING TO KNOW YOUR UNDERLYING DREAMS AND ASPIRATIONS

So is it possible to meet some of these underlying needs in a dream job without sacrificing the things you really care about? Certainly!

There are all *sorts* of aspirations that can satisfy your key needs without compromising the things you *care* about. So below are a few for you to think about; these are based on what a large body of research (as well as our grandparents' wisdom!) shows are key to a happy life:

▶ **Master a craft.** One very healthy aspiration is to become really good at something you enjoy – whether through university or otherwise. You might not know what that thing is today, but having this goal in mind over the long term can set you up well for the future. When you become really good at something you enjoy, not only does your work become more fulfilling, you're also more likely to make a good living off it. Specialist skills have a habit of being very well-paid.

▶ **Contribute to a community that you care about.** People who help others often get a lot of satisfaction, and joy, from doing so. Examples include volunteer work, political activism and other forms of community service. Such activities promote mental wellbeing and are worth considering in whatever path you choose. They're also a great opportunity to meet other people who care about the same social issues as you.

▶ **Recognise the importance of time with friends and family.** Prioritising time with family and friends might not be at the forefront of your mind right now, especially if it feels like you have all the time in the world for your friends, and/or you feel like you would like to get some independence from your family for a while! But psychologists are unanimous that one of the keys to a happy life is meaningful social relationships. So, as you think about what you'd like do, and where you'd like to go, after school, also think about how your decision will affect how you stay in touch with those you care about the most.

Alternative Perspective
Tony Hawk, professional skateboarder

Tony Hawk is an iconic professional skateboarder who, from a young age, focussed relentlessly on mastering his sport. He never went to university, and reflecting on his career and success in an interview, he once highlighted a perspective that I think is worth considering when thinking about careers:

'I try to tell people [that] you don't have to be the best in your field to enjoy it [and] make a living at it. You can find some angle on it... [that] gets you in the door and you get to be part of the community or the industry, and you can live like that... Think of something that you would enjoy, and make that your job, because for me that's what success is.'

Your underlying life aspirations are likely to change as you grow, and that can also change how you think about your dream career – and this is perfectly normal. Ultimately, only you can decide what matters to you at each stage of your life. If you're mindful about your deeper aspirations and motivations *now*, you will be in a better position to choose and build a career that's more aligned with who you really are.

Chapter Recap

▶ Whether you know what you would like to do after school or not, it's useful to reflect on your underlying aspirations and motivations. They'll help you to paint a picture in your head of many possible bright futures, which can broaden your prospects.

▶ Once you have some ideas about your deeper aspirations, you can use them as a starting point to explore a range of careers that can fulfil them – and the educational paths that could lead you there.

▶ Knowing your aspirations means you can sense-check them. Watch out for tempting, but possibly distracting or restricting aspirations, such as money and fame, and consider aspirations that free you up and widen your possibilities instead. Such aspirations may include helping and caring for others, using your creative abilities, or the pursuit of a specific skill that you can master.

Part One: Conclusion

My hope is that Part One has provided you with a healthy foundation from which to tackle your decision of what to do after school – a foundation based on three main suggestions:

1. Aim for a good decision, rather than a perfect one.

2. Use the decision-making process as an opportunity to think independently and critically, and to make confident, self-empowering choices for yourself.

3. Be mindful of your deeper aspirations in life. Some will allow you to think more freely about your future; others may distract you from doing what's truly right for you.

With the foundation of Part One in place, we can now dive into the more practical sections of the book. In Part Two we'll therefore look at the two most popular and established educational routes after school (University and Apprenticeships), as well two alternative paths (Working Your Way Up and Taking Time Out to Think).

PART TWO
POSSIBLE PATHS

What are the realities of going to university? Do apprenticeships offer a strong enough alternative to a degree? And what else can you do if neither of those routes suits you?

This section will answer these questions and more. In particular, it will:

▶ help to give you a realistic perspective on university

▶ demystify apprenticeships, and

▶ provide a starting point on how to think about the options of going straight into work or taking a gap year.

4
GOING TO UNIVERSITY

Every year more than half a million people in the UK apply to go to university. It has become the most common school-leaver route for a range of reasons, but the motivation for most people is simple: the notion that a university degree promises to improve your career prospects. As a result, more than ever, young people today opt for university as the default path. Let's look at a few figures that back this up.

In the 2020/21 UCAS application cycle, over 40% of 18-year-olds in the UK – the highest number on record at the time – applied to enrol on a university course starting in 2021. If this age band is expanded to cover people aged 17 to 30, it reveals that over half of all people in that age group opt to go to university.

In contrast, there's probably only around 7–10% of 18-year-olds who take the apprenticeship path. One reason that this percentage is so much lower is that there are significantly more university places than there are apprenticeships. (In 2019/20, there were three times more university places taken up by people aged 19 or younger than there were apprenticeships taken up by the same age group.) However, another reason is that apprenticeships can be overlooked as a viable choice because the university path is more widely thought of, and promoted, as the 'better' choice.

Such attitudes will hopefully evolve in the future. But for now, many people see a degree as the best way of getting a qualification beyond school. It's also important to note that there are some areas where a specialist degree is required, such as those in the table below:

Occupation areas	Examples of jobs that require specialist degrees
Construction	• Architect • Building Control officer • Civil engineer
Medicine and Healthcare	• Doctor • Dentist • Psychologist
Education	• Teacher • Professor • University lecturer
Sciences	• Aerospace engineer • Astronomer • Marine biologist

Besides the specialist professions in the table above, you can find a degree in nearly anything you're interested in. Fancy taking your passion for baking to a professional level? If so, you can apply for a Baking Technology degree that provides you with an applied skill set and teaches you the science and business of the industry.

If you prefer a more traditional university education with broader academic learning, you can mix your interests with combination degrees, such as the famous Philosophy, Politics and Economics course (better known as PPE), or you can opt for a Joint Honours programme that allows you to study more than one subject. You can even mix science and arts subjects, by choosing the likes of Engineering with French. The best resource for the wide range of courses on offer can be found at *www.ucas.com/explore/subjects*.

University has proved time and again that it can, of course, lead to professional success. According to a 2019 report by educational charity the Sutton Trust, around nine out of ten people in influential positions in society, whether that's politicians, CEOs of large companies, or leaders in the media, went to university.

But does university work that well for everyone? And is it really the main factor that leads to professional success? Or could there be other factors at play in landing such influential positions, regardless of whether you go to university or not? We'll return to these ideas in later chapters, but first, let's look at what university requires from you (other than the fees of course, which we cover in Chapter 10); whether it prepares you for work; and how well it delivers on one of its major promises today: landing you a good job.

What's University Like and What's Expected of You?

Undergraduate degrees are typically three years long, but most graduates agree that time at university seems to just fly by. On top of the workload of lectures, tutorials, assignment deadlines and exams, there's also a lot to keep you busy outside the lecture halls – from all the social events to all the extracurricular activities that Student Unions and societies offer. So much so that you may find yourself wishing you had just a little more time!

Thankfully, most university courses don't count the grades you get in your first year as part of the final degree grade. (Or in some cases they give it the lowest weighting in your overall degree classification.) This gives you time to settle into a course and adjust to a workload that's a step-up from A levels. It's only when you get to the second year and beyond that you generally start to experience the real demands of a degree.

Insight

A sample week in the life of a university student

University life is a little different for everyone. However, most of your time is spent on academic learning – either in lectures and tutorials, or on your own in self-study. Here's what a week might look like for a Business Management course student who is also a member of the Debating Society:

Monday
- 9:00 to 11:00 – Microeconomics lecture
- 11:00 to 13:00 – Break
- 13:00 to 14:30 – Introduction to Marketing lecture
- 14:30 to 16:30 – Break
- 16:30 to 18:00 – Accounting lecture

Tuesday
- 9:00 to 11:00 – Strategy lecture
- 11:00 to 15:00 – Break
- 15:00 to 16:00 – Macroeconomics lecture
- 16:00 to 17:00 – Break
- 17:00 to 18:30 – Corporate Finance lecture

Wednesday
- No lectures
- 10:00 to 13:00 – Studying in library

CHAPTER 4 GOING TO UNIVERSITY

The demands of a degree

The majority of learning at university – which is mostly academic rather than practical (more on this in Chapter 9) – happens in lectures. According to 'The Uni Guide' (www.theuniguide.co.uk), the average weekly teaching time at university in the UK is around 14 hours per week, although that can vary by subject.

The chart on page 50 shows that Creative Writing students have an average of nine hours of teaching per week; Business Management students around 12 hours; Computer Science students 15 hours;

- 13:00 to 19:00 – Time off
- 19:00 to 22:00 – Student Union drinks with the debating society

Thursday
- 10:00 to 12:30 – Economics tutorial
- 12:30 to 13:30 – Break
- 13:30 to 14:30 – Information Technology workshop
- 14:30 to 16:30 – Break
- 16:30 to 18:00 – Corporate Finance tutorial
- 18:00 to 18:30 – Break
- 18:30 to 19:00 – Employer presentation and recruitment event

Friday
- 9:00 to 11:00 – Studying in library
- 11:00 to 12:30 – Break
- 12:30 to 14:30 – Debating society meeting
- 14:30 to 16:30 – Leadership lecture
- 16:30 to 17:00 – Break
- 17:00 to 18:00 – Strategy lecture

Saturday
- Day off

Sunday
- Day off

while Chemistry, Medicine, Nursing and Physics students have an average of around or just above 20 hours.

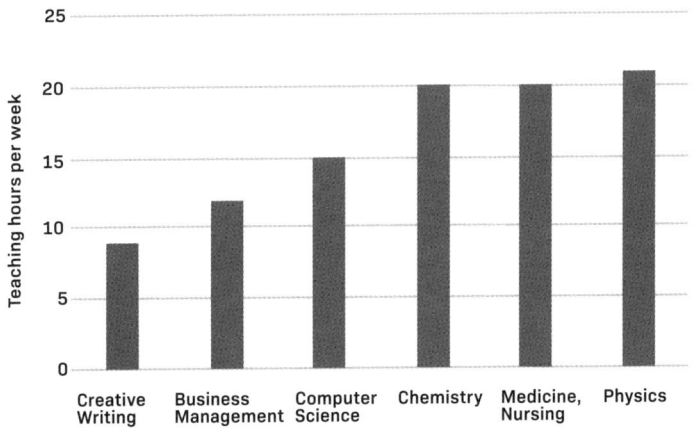

(Data Source: The Uni Guide)

In addition to teaching hours, you are expected to study independently. Some courses, such as Chemistry, Medicine, Nursing and Physics, can demand another 20-plus hours per week of independent study. So for these subjects, it isn't unusual to find students who spend over 40 hours per week studying.

While study hours vary from subject to subject, figures like the ones above hopefully highlight that university is by no means a walk in the park. Students who really want to get the best out of the uni experience spend a lot of their time in lectures and just as many, if not more, studying independently.

CHAPTER 4 GOING TO UNIVERSITY

Insight
How many hours should you commit to university?

To get what is considered a good degree classification – i.e. either a First (the highest honours awarded) or a 2.1 (pronounced 'two-one' – the second highest honours awarded) – most people need to dedicate around 30–40 hours per week to university learning, which isn't all that different to what you'd expect with a full-time job. Spending less time than this on your studies is unlikely to yield the academic results that will make you stand out when you graduate.

The chart below shows the average workload of a number of subjects according to a 2021 survey by the Higher Education Policy Institute. Note that these are averages, so they won't necessarily reflect how much time you need to invest based on your personal circumstances. However, they can be a useful indication of roughly what to expect.

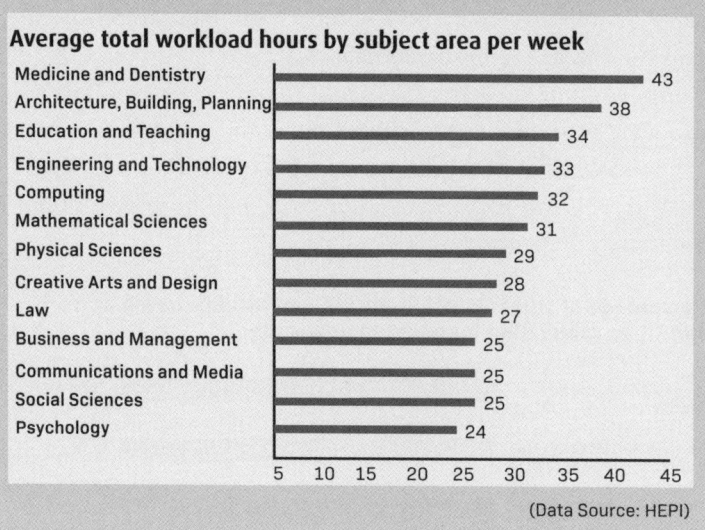

Average total workload hours by subject area per week

Medicine and Dentistry	43
Architecture, Building, Planning	38
Education and Teaching	34
Engineering and Technology	33
Computing	32
Mathematical Sciences	31
Physical Sciences	29
Creative Arts and Design	28
Law	27
Business and Management	25
Communications and Media	25
Social Sciences	25
Psychology	24

(Data Source: HEPI)

Does University Prepare You for Work?

Doing a degree will nurture skills that serve you well long after you graduate, no matter what type of work you go on to do. For example, university study helps to develop research skills, analytical abilities and enhanced critical thinking – all skills that can be applied in almost any job, and that will help you succeed in life after school.

That said, the university experience doesn't just have to be about preparation for the world of work. Studying a subject at degree level can be rewarding in its own right too – from an intellectual perspective. After all, there's value in learning for learning's sake – as well as in learning a subject well enough to potentially contribute to academic research in that field.

However, as shown in the chart below, the number one reason that people choose to go to university is to advance their careers, which is why the focus here is on how well a degree prepares someone for the world of work.

Percentage of students who selected a particular reason as a top-three motivation for going to university

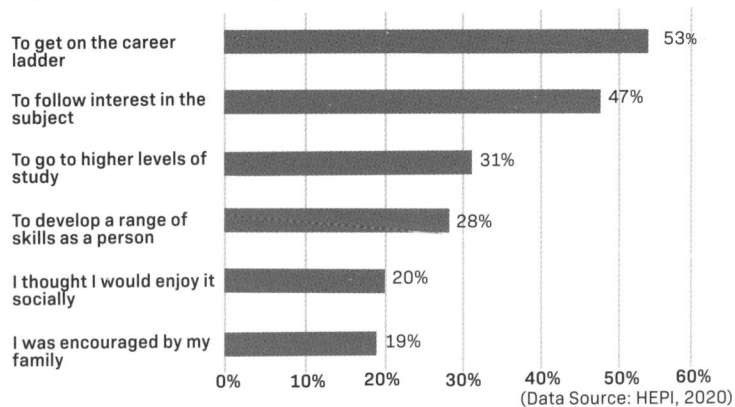

(Data Source: HEPI, 2020)

Graduate Perspective

Anthony Spencer, Sports Science Graduate (now a Project Management Consultant)

Anthony did a degree in Sports Science but later on transitioned into a project management career in the financial services industry. His experience is one of many examples of how a degree in one subject area can still offer skills that are useful elsewhere. His advice to young people is simple:

> 'If you want to do a job where you learn a specific skill and apply it, for example, computer programming, chef skills, emergency service work, childcare or adventure activity guidance, there are likely to be [specific] industry certifications and qualifications that will help you much more than university. For other, less specialised jobs, a bachelor's degree can provide the transferable skills [required].'

A few examples of the many areas of work where any degree can be relevant are: management consultancy, civil service work, journalism, charity fundraising, and marketing.

When we start to really look at how well a degree prepares students for work though, it turns out that a university education has limits that are felt by both graduates and employers. A 2020 survey by the graduate jobs website www.milkround.com revealed that a majority of graduates felt somewhat or mostly unprepared for the workplace. In fact, just 15% felt completely prepared by their degree. In addition, a survey by Pearson Business School in 2019 found that employers felt that nearly one in five graduates are not ready for the workplace. One of the key failings reported was that, although university is well-equipped to teach *conceptual* knowledge, it doesn't do so well at teaching more practical work and life skills, such as negotiation, leadership, problem solving, adaptability and applied creativity.

It would seem that this kind of practical knowledge is better acquired *outside* the classroom – through 'doing' things in everyday life, rather than just through studying.

It is, however, possible to make up for this shortcoming while at university by arranging work experience alongside your degree. Some students take up part-time work during term-time or full-time roles during the holidays. Another way of getting valuable work experience is through an internship or a sandwich degree (a regular degree but with a substantial work placement in between your studies) – both of which give you specific subject-related experience. Any of these options will help you graduate both with academic rigour *and* with practical, real-world experience that you wouldn't have secured through study alone.

What are the Employment Prospects of Graduates?

Even though university is far from perfect when it comes to preparing you for the world of work, it does nonetheless generally lead to high-quality employment.

Historically, around 70% of UK university graduates are in full-time or part-time work within a year or so of graduating. More precisely, the Higher Education Statistics Agency (HESA) reported in 2020 that almost 60% of people with an undergraduate degree were in full-time jobs within 15 months of graduating; around 10% were in part-time roles, 20% were in further studies (for example, a master's degree), and only 4% were unemployed.

Just as encouraging is the high proportion of employed graduates who are in high- or medium-skill professions, such as managers or technical professionals. Almost 80% of recently employed graduates were in these types of jobs.

These statistics have held up well over the long term, too. When you consider the general adult UK working population, you find that almost 90% of graduates are employed, and within that working group, around 70% are in high-skilled jobs.

The UK government publishes this data every year for graduates living in England, and consistently finds that degree-holders are more likely to be employed than non-graduates. You can see this pattern in the chart below (although it's worth noting that their data doesn't consider highly skilled apprentices, whose employment prospects are actually just as good).

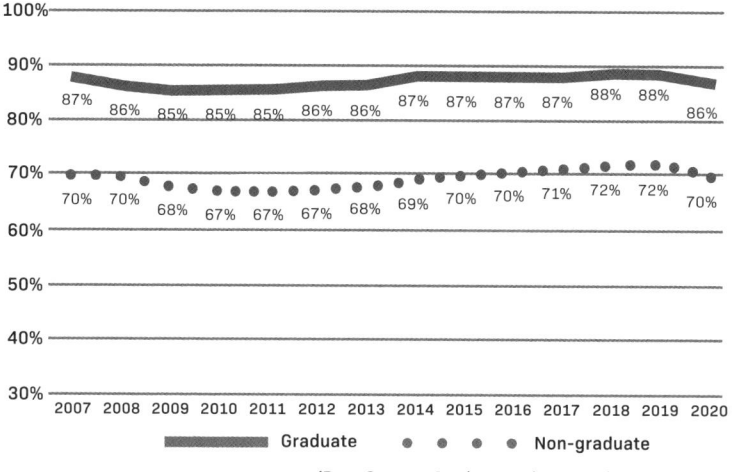

(Data Source: Graduate Labour Market Statistics)

The nuances of employment prospect rates

As you might expect, you shouldn't take the statistics for graduate employment prospects too literally since prospects are not the same for everyone. Factors such as the state of the economy when you graduate, the quality of the university you attend, the grade you achieve and the degree subject you study, all play a role.

One stark example of how the statistics need to be broken down to show a more grounded picture is that, while over 80% of Medicine and Dentistry graduates secure roles not long after graduation, just 40–50% of Law, History, Philosophy and Creative Arts undergraduates do so.

It's important to make an exception for Medicine courses though, as university places for Medicine are restricted by the government since it costs relatively more to train doctors. Yet their skills are

> **Insight**
> **The impact of the COVID-19 pandemic on 2020/21 graduates**
>
> Historically, long-term graduate employment rates have been good. But the impact of the global Covid-19 pandemic since early 2020 on the economy meant that employment rates in 2020 were severely affected (the same applied to apprenticeships, though data here is more limited). For example, a 2020 survey by the graduate careers website www.prospects.ac.uk found that:
>
> - 29% of final-year students lost the jobs they had while at university
> - 26% of students lost their internships or work placements
> - 28% of those with graduate job offers had their contracts deferred or cancelled.
>
> The *Financial Times* surveyed the graduating class of 2021 and found that many graduates had to take jobs that paid less than they had hoped for, while half of degree-holders felt that the pandemic had set back their career prospects. So what can you do if you find your options dwindling in an economic downturn? Here are a few useful tips to keep in mind:

always in high demand, which means they are almost always guaranteed a job.

Despite this quirk of Medicine, there's a point worth uncovering here – and that's that employment rates are often driven by how many skilled graduates are available to fill a particular role. And so for some courses, such as Law or Business, finding employment is more competitive since there are significantly more graduates in those subjects than there are job vacancies.

Still, going to university can safely be considered an overall good bet when it to comes to enhancing employment prospects – as long as you make the most of the whole experience!

- **Be adaptable** – The *Financial Times* survey mentioned earlier found that more than a third of the 2021 graduates were forced to change their intended career direction as a result of the pandemic; however, they didn't all see this as a negative. For some, the pandemic provided an opportunity to reassess whether the subject and careers they were pursuing were truly right for them. For example, the technology sector thrived in the pandemic, which means that some non-tech graduates shifted in this direction, applying for roles in areas such as digital marketing, data science and logistics.
- **Be optimistic** – Try to remember that, although things may feel tough, no economic downturn lasts forever, so things *will* change eventually. In the meantime, try to look for a silver lining somewhere. For instance, should you find yourself out of work, look for opportunities to pick up new skills while you have the time. This might, for example, involve free online learning or voluntary work experience (as some students did by supporting the healthcare sector at the height of the pandemic).
- **Ask for help** – If you're really struggling, don't be afraid to ask for help. Beyond friends and family, if you are at university, you can contact the Student Union welfare team, or organisations such as the Nightline Association (www.nightline.ac.uk).

> ## Insight
> ### How to boost your graduate job prospects
>
> - **Internships**. Graduate employers tend to favour candidates who have some work experience under their belt. So if you go to university, try to get some form of work experience, either during the holidays or part-time during term time. Ideally, this would be a role that's linked to an industry that you would like to enter after graduation or that will, at least, give you some relevant insights.
>
> - **Academic grades**. Most employers ask for a minimum of a 2.1 degree, so it helps to achieve this grade or higher. The important thing here is to make sure that your university efforts reflect what you're truly capable of. In other words, don't slack off!
>
> - **Non-academic pursuits**. As the graduate population grows, it's important to make yourself stand out in ways beyond just your academic ability. For example, you might want to get involved in a university society, volunteer with a charity, or work on a side-project that shows off your creative talents. Whatever you choose, try to do something that will distinguish you from others in some way and therefore prevent you from being 'just another graduate'.

An Overview of University

By now, you'll have gathered that going to university can indeed lead to positive career outcomes. And that, while doing a degree can be challenging, it also helps you to develop skills such as critical thinking, which are transferable to many careers. This is part of the reason why graduates have high employment rates compared to students who don't go on to do any further training or education after school.

CHAPTER 4 GOING TO UNIVERSITY

University is also a place where you can grow as a person and become more confident in your individuality; and it's an environment where you will meet and make friends with people from all over the UK, and potentially from all over the world. University campuses are rich in diversity of backgrounds and cultures, which makes them a great environment for expanding your worldviews and encouraging respect for people's differences. These are among the many positives that cannot always be found in the workplace.

With all that said, you have to remember that, despite being a well-established path after school, going to university by no means *guarantees* career success. To do well, you have to invest a lot of effort in your studies and, ideally, complement them with practical work experience. This practical side of learning is something that apprenticeships are better at offering, so we'll turn to that in the next chapter.

Chapter Recap

▶ University is a popular choice because of its potential to improve career prospects. Doing a degree can also be intellectually rewarding in its own right.

▶ To get the most of out of university, students generally have to spend around 30 to 40 hours a week doing academic work, which means it can be just as demanding as a full-time job.

▶ Overall, university boosts employment prospects: 70% of graduates find work (most of which is high-skilled) shortly after graduating.

▶ University is a great place to develop transferable life skills, such as critical thinking, research techniques and analytical abilities. It's also a good environment to grow as an individual, but delivers less on advancing *practical* knowledge.

▶ A majority of UK graduates report that university didn't prepare them well for their careers, so it's hugely beneficial to secure relevant work experience in the real world before or while completing a degree.

5
DOING AN APPRENTICESHIP

Although apprenticeships might seem new to some, they've been around for hundreds of years. From medieval times, young people would often train with experts to master practical skills. And when that training was done, the apprentice would typically join a union of professionals whose standards were upheld by some central authority.

Apprenticeship methods still thrive today. They're everywhere (both formally and informally) if you look close enough – from the winners of the BBC's *The Apprentice* competition, who receive mentorship from the seasoned businessman Lord Alan Sugar, to gamers who master Fortnite by imitating more experienced players on YouTube.

Even graduates who take up a job after university undergo an unspoken form of apprenticeship at their new workplace – learning through real-world practice, with guidance from an expert until they can do tasks on their own. This way of learning is how most people acquire new skills.

Despite how widespread the model of *informal* apprenticeship learning is, formal apprenticeships are, unfortunately, still mostly associated with a limited set of skilled trades such as hairdressing, plumbing and construction work. But this thinking is out of date, as, in recent times, a much broader range of formal apprenticeships have emerged to cater for a variety of career choices.

World-renowned designer Alexander McQueen completed an apprenticeship in fashion, for example; celebrity chef Jamie Oliver completed an NVQ in home economics before apprenticing at several restaurants; the Managing Director of Formula One, Ross Brawn, completed an apprenticeship in mechanical engineering; and politician Gillian Keegan did one in manufacturing before her business career and later election as Chichester's first female Member of Parliament.

Apprenticeships are now proving to be an attractive alternative to university: you get paid to train rather than having to pay to learn. And although apprenticeships are still a minority option, by 2021 the more advanced apprenticeship offering (better known as the Higher Apprenticeship) had five times as many new trainees in England compared to six years earlier. As we'll find in later chapters, this level of training can reap similar financial rewards to those that university graduates often enjoy.

> **Insight**
> **You don't need a degree to qualify as a solicitor**
>
> Did you know that you don't always need to go to university to become a solicitor? In 2020, the Solicitors Regulation Authority (SRA) in England and Wales made changes to the qualification process so that an apprenticeship path with a law firm is also possible. This means that aspiring solicitors can 'earn as they learn', rather than spend over £50,000 in fees and costs on the traditional university path. You can learn more about this at www.sra.org.uk/students/sqe/solicitor-apprenticeships.

CHAPTER 5 DOING AN APPRENTICESHIP

Apprentice Perspective

Haider Ali, Higher Level Apprentice in Management Accounting at Rolls-Royce

We met Haider in Chapter 2. His parents supported his decision to pursue an apprenticeship after his uncle vouched for the credibility of this path. However, Haider was personally convinced long before that. Even though he was predicted (and achieved) A*s and As in his A levels, and secured offers at top universities, as soon as he learnt about apprenticeships, the right route for him became obvious:

> 'It was completely new to me. I'd never really considered or even met an apprentice prior to sixth form. I thought it was kind of a GCSE equivalent, so in my mind, and in my parents' minds, an apprenticeship meant almost going backwards – I'd almost be going back to GCSE level. It didn't make sense.

> 'But then I came across things like Degree Apprenticeships and Higher Apprenticeships. That's when I started to find out that there are apprenticeship levels all the way up to a degree and master's equivalent. I was thinking, "This sounds great – you're getting paid work experience, no debt, and you can work with some really high-profile companies, which looks great on your CV."

> 'But then I guess part of me was also a bit paranoid. It seemed like a win-win, but what's the catch? Why aren't more people doing this? And I guess there wasn't really a catch, to be honest. I think it's just the fact that herd behaviour is so prevalent within schools that even if something is glaringly obvious, and amazing for you, people think there's something wrong with it just because not enough people have done it.'

The negative stereotypes of apprenticeships being in some way 'lesser' than uni degrees are also now starting to vanish. For example, a survey by the educational charity Demos found that over 90% of parents now believe apprenticeships are a 'good option' for young people. And a 2021 poll by *The Times* and

YouGov found that 42% of people believed that an apprenticeship was better at preparing young people for their future than university; this was seven times higher than the proportion of people who believed a university degree would provide better preparation for life.

More employers are now also introducing apprenticeship routes into professional roles at their firms. This includes some of the UK's biggest employers, such as Amazon, Coca-Cola, Morrisons, the Royal Air Force and HSBC.

But do modern apprenticeships really have what it takes to be a strong contender to a university degree? From a career perspective, I believe that they do. So in this chapter, we'll dig into how apprenticeships work and consider the impact they can have on your career.

How Modern Apprenticeships Work

Apprenticeships today tend to be well established and well structured, unlike in previous generations where the quality of training was less consistent. Regulation is such that the word 'Apprenticeship' now has similar legal recognition to the word 'Degree'. Under The Enterprise Act (2016) in UK law, employers and training providers may only offer an 'apprenticeship' if strict government standards are met. This means that you can have confidence that apprenticeships are designed with quality in mind.

So how do apprenticeships work? There will always be some variation between employers, but the basic idea across all schemes is a combination of paid work and on-the-job training. Here's what you can expect.

Apprenticeship levels: an introduction to the lingo

First, the basics. Anyone who is aged 16 or over, but isn't in full-time education, can apply for an apprenticeship. However, each apprenticeship 'level' has different entry qualification requirements in terms of GCSEs or A levels.

The table below highlights the four basic types of apprenticeships available in England. These are broadly known as Intermediate, Advanced, Higher and Degree Apprenticeships. As you'll see from the table, after your A levels, you can qualify for a Higher or Degree Apprenticeship.

Apprenticeship Level (National Qualification Level)	Education Equivalent	Academic Entry Requirements	Length
Intermediate (Level 2)	5 GCSEs	Usually no academic requirements, but some employers ask for English and Maths GCSEs	12 months
Advanced (Level 3)	2 A levels	2-5 GCSEs	18-24 months
Higher (Levels 4 & 5)	Foundation Degree	A levels or equivalent qualifications	2-3 years
Degree Apprenticeship (Levels 6 & 7)	Bachelor's or Master's Degree	Strong A level grades	3-5 years

If you live in Scotland, Wales or Northern Ireland, you'll find slightly different versions of these levels. Refer to the websites below for information about these regions.
- ▶ **Scotland**

  www.apprenticeships.scot/become-an-apprentice
- ▶ **Wales**

  https://gov.wales/become-apprentice
- ▶ **Northern Ireland**

  www.nidirect.gov.uk/campaigns/apprenticeships

Insight
The option of Degree Apprenticeships

Degree Apprenticeships are an alternative to traditional apprenticeships, in that they still involve on-the-job learning, but also have a significant academic component. At the end of the programme, you will walk away with a university degree (paid for by your employer), substantial work experience and, in most cases, the opportunity to continue working with your employer.

Degree Apprenticeships are available in England and Wales. In Scotland there is a similar scheme called a Graduate Apprenticeship. And in Northern Ireland, where the programmes are relatively new, they are also called Degree Apprenticeships. Sample subjects include Business, Engineering, Computer Science, Data Science and Nursing. The programmes are typically run by an employer in partnership with a university, allowing you to spend part of your training in a work setting and part in an academic setting – at university.

However, as appealing as they might be, there is generally more competition for Degree Apprenticeships than for university placements and traditional apprenticeships, since vacancies are in smaller numbers. For example, in February 2021, only around 300 vacancies were advertised in England – on the government website www.apprenticeships.gov.uk. New vacancies are added every month though, and in the three years leading up to 2021, each year saw around 4,000 to 5,000 vacancies in England alone.

If you think you would enjoy a hybrid of academic study and practical work experience, a Degree Apprenticeship might be worth investigating. Just be sure that, if you decide to go for this option, you have a back-up plan (such as university offers or other apprenticeship schemes), given how competitive this route is.

Where to learn more about Degree Apprenticeships:
- **England** *www.gov.uk/government/publications/higher-and-degree-apprenticeships*
- **Wales** *https://careerswales.gov.wales/apprenticeships/degree-apprenticeships*
- **Scotland** – *www.apprenticeships.scot/become-an-apprentice/graduate-apprenticeships*
- **Northern Ireland** *www.nidirect.gov.uk/articles/higher-level-apprenticeships*

CHAPTER 5 DOING AN APPRENTICESHIP

Degree Apprentice Perspective

Freya Woodward, Degree Apprentice (now a Project Manager at Arcadis)

The usual path to a Degree Apprenticeship is to apply directly to an employer. But Freya Woodward, who now works as a Project Manager at the global engineering firm Arcadis, took a different approach. Freya got some work experience first, applied and got on to a traditional degree course, and then later converted to a Degree Apprenticeship for her final years. Here's how she recalls her journey:

'I decided, actually before I'd even got my [A level] results, that I wasn't going to go to university straightaway. I ended up working in South Africa and Swaziland for a bit, and then came back to the UK to start my degree course.

'I [then] – like a lot of students – got a part-time job, but I got one with a construction company so that I was learning at the same time as working. I also wanted to make the most of the university experience and all the things the university had to offer. I went on trips with the university; I was part of the air squadron and a lot of societies and clubs; and I did a lot of advocating for the university.

'It sounds very intense looking back: I was at uni two days a week, working in an office three days a week, and an RAF reserve for two days at the weekend. They're three very different things, but I feel I got the most out of my uni experience.

'After two years I was [then] given an option to either do a year-out placement or convert onto an apprenticeship programme for my final two years, which would mean that my degree would be paid for. So I converted and did the last two years of my degree as an apprenticeship.'

The work: what do you actually do as an apprentice?

Apprentices in the UK can choose from over a thousand different occupations in 170-plus industries. When they join an organisation, they do so as a full-time employee and work for 30 to 40 hours per week (inclusive of training time). Apprentices also get full employment rights, such as paid holidays and sick pay.

The table opposite shows a range of professions that apprentices can pursue, and the table that then follows that highlights some of the leading apprenticeship employers according to the National Apprenticeship Service (www.apprenticeships.gov.uk). See also pages 70–71 for a more comprehensive list of the kind of apprenticeships available in the UK.

Apprentices are trained in a real-world setting where knowledge and learning is applied daily. They are tasked with real responsibilities, from working on major construction projects, dealing with customer queries at a bank, through to supporting a team of consultants in drafting a strategy report for a client, depending on the area of work, of course.

Taking the apprenticeship path requires sustained effort, as they can take between one and five years depending on the path you choose. However, at the end of the training, you will receive a qualification that is recognised nationally.

Example professions that apprentices can pursue

Occupation areas/ example apprenticeship	Suitability
Business and Law	
• Accounting • Banking • Finance • Law	If you're interested in business, entrepreneurship and/or finance
Health and Public Services	
• Civil servant • Nursing • Military and defence	If you wish to serve in a public capacity
Engineering	
• Telecoms engineering • Computer science • Mechanical engineering	If you enjoy building and/or designing things
Media and Publishing	
• Journalism • TV and Radio • Internet advertising	If you're a creative media enthusiast
Science and Mathematics	
• Pharmaceuticals • Biomedical sciences • Psychology	If you enjoy maths or science, but would prefer a more practical approach to learning

Examples from the Top 100 Apprenticeship Employers list (as compiled by the National Apprenticeship Service)

Organisation	Number of apprentices recruited (1 April 2019–31 March 2020)
British Army	8,419

The British Army is ranked number one in the top 100 apprenticeship employers. Around one in five employees in the army are on the apprenticeship path, and training programmes aren't just about becoming a soldier either. There are roles in Health, Engineering, Telecommunications, IT and Construction. The Army also offer a Degree Apprenticeship that leads to a BA (Hons) in Business Leadership and Management.

You can learn more at *https://apply.army.mod.uk*.

BT	2,887

BT is a telecommunications company with over 100,000 employees. It provides TV and phone services, as well as broadband internet. It is the number one *private* sector employer of apprentices. Roles are available across Digital services, Engineering, Customer service, Cyber Security and Marketing. Starting salaries for apprentices here are around £16,000 per year. Although the business recruited almost 3,000 apprentices in 2019/20, this number fell to around 230 in 2021.

You can learn more at *www.bt.com/careers/early-careers/apprentices*.

Royal Navy	2,774

The Royal Navy has an 'outstanding' rating from education inspectors Ofsted. It offers roles in Aviation, Logistics, Engineering, Human resources, IT and Communications. If you have strong A levels and are interested in engineering, you may want to consider an Accelerated Apprenticeship as a technician, where you can earn £31,000 a year. There's also a Degree Apprenticeship route in Engineering, where you get paid up to £45,000 a year (this route requires a minimum of 48 UCAS points and qualifications in Maths, Science or Engineering).

You can learn more at *www.royalnavy.mod.uk/careers/levels-of-entry/apprenticeships*.

PwC	946

PwC (also known as PricewaterhouseCoopers) is a business consulting and accounting firm with a global network of offices.

The business has several Higher Apprenticeship opportunities across its key business lines of Advisory (i.e. consulting), Assurance (i.e. accounting and audit services), and Tax. Students who join the Assurance or Tax departments get free training to qualify as Chartered Accountants.

CHAPTER 5 DOING AN APPRENTICESHIP

Network Rail   673

Almost 5 million people travel every day on railway tracks that are owned and managed by Network Rail – an organisation owned and funded by the UK government. Network Rail offer apprenticeships in Finance, Engineering and Operations. Degree Apprenticeships are on offer in IT and Business Services, with a starting salary of £17,000.

You can learn more at *www.networkrail.co.uk/careers/early-careers/apprenticeships*.

NHS   Figures not available

The National Health Service (NHS) employs just over 1.2 million people and is one of the largest employers in the world. The NHS recruits on a regular basis and offers all levels of apprenticeships. Roles include Ambulance Practitioner, Nursing, Dental Nursing, and Leader and Management apprenticeships.

You can learn more at *www.healthcareers.nhs.uk/career-planning/study-and-training/apprenticeships*.

Unilever   260

Unilever is a British consumer goods business with 149,000 employees and operations across the world. They are known for brands such as Dove, Hellmann's and Persil. Unilever has apprenticeships all the way to degree level, and they are focussed on three areas: Business and Technology (for example, project management, cybersecurity and data science), Research and Development (for scientific and engineering qualifications), and Supply Chain (for example, planning and quality, and supply chain management).

You can learn more at *https://careers.unilever.com*.

Other well-known employers who take on a smaller number of apprentices include:

Facebook This is one of the world's largest technology businesses. It owns WhatsApp, Instagram and the virtual reality business Oculus VR. Apprenticeships at Facebook are usually focussed on Software Engineering. They are extremely competitive and require top A level results that benefit from having at least one maths, science or technology subject. You can learn more at *www.facebook.com/careers*.

BBC The British Broadcasting Corporation employs over 20,000 people. It has apprenticeship programmes in Journalism, TV Production and Business Management, as well as Design and Engineering. You can learn more at *www.bbc.co.uk/careers/trainee-schemes-and-apprenticeships*.

AstraZeneca This is a global pharmaceutical company that led the way with a COVID-19 vaccine in 2020 and 2021. It employs over 70,000 people and today has a wide range of apprenticeships that span Science and Laboratory work, IT and Data, Business and Operations Management. Degree Apprenticeships are also available for areas that require a degree-level of specialism. You can learn more at *careers.astrazeneca.com/early-talent*.

Find the complete list at *www.topapprenticeshipemployers.co.uk*.

The training: how do apprentices learn?

While most learning as an apprentice happens 'on-the-job', every apprenticeship includes at least 20% of time on 'off-the-job' study. This includes online classes, attending a local college/university, or going to a specific training facility within the company itself.

Practically, this can be structured in different ways. For example, if your apprenticeship hours are 35 hours per week (seven hours per day, Monday to Friday), you might spend four days a week in the workplace and one day a week studying. Alternatively, an employer might provide the 20% training in one block each month – so 16 days at work and four days of back-to-back training. Or they might provide the training all in one go – in a set separate period during the year. In all scenarios, you will be paid for both your workplace and your study hours.

> **Insight**
> **Off-the-job training versus on-the-job training**
>
> As we have just seen, apprentices learn by a combination of doing a job practically (on-the-job learning) and studying outside of work (off-the-job learning). The Education and Skills Funding Agency in the UK has more precise definitions for these two processes. Here's an extract from their 2021 guidance for employers and trainers:
>
> 'Off-the-job training is a statutory requirement for an English apprenticeship. It is training which is received by the apprentice, during the apprentice's normal working hours, for the purpose of achieving the knowledge, skills and behaviours of the approved apprenticeship referenced in the apprenticeship agreement. By normal working hours we mean the hours for which the apprentice would normally be paid, excluding overtime.
>
> 'It is not on-the-job training which is training received by the apprentice for the sole purpose of enabling the apprentice to perform the work for which they have been employed. By this we mean training that does not specifically link to the knowledge, skills and behaviours set out in the apprenticeship agreement.'

CHAPTER 5 DOING AN APPRENTICESHIP

The purpose of the combination of workplace training and academic study is to arm you with the knowledge, skills and behaviours that are set out in the apprenticeship agreement.

Every apprentice has to complete assessments before becoming fully qualified. Depending on the specific programme, these can include technical tests and exams, and role-playing and simulation tests, as well as a professional discussion where an independent assessor asks you open-ended questions about your work. Such rigorous assessment ensures that, at the end of an apprenticeship, you have what it takes to succeed in your profession.

The pay: is it good enough?

A key benefit of the apprenticeship route is the opportunity to start earning right away. So instead of taking out a government loan to cover your university tuition fees, you'll be paid to work and train. Starting salaries for Higher and Degree apprenticeships can range from £15,000 to £30,000 a year.

Pay levels depend on several factors: the specific apprenticeship you're taking, the industry you're in and the geographical region of employment (for example London firms usually pay a bit more than regional ones). At the very least, an employer must meet the minimum wage rates set out in the table on page 74. These figures apply from April 2022, but be sure to check www.gov.uk/national-minimum-wage-rates for the latest rates.

It's important to note that first-year apprentices have a lower minimum wage compared to other groups. But this can increase significantly (depending on your age) once you enter into the second year of your apprenticeship. In addition, many employers pay more than the minimum wage because they want to attract the best talent. This is evident from government surveys of apprenticeship pay. A report published in 2020, for example, revealed that the average hourly wage for a Higher Apprenticeship was £12.46 per hour. The annual equivalent salary here would be around £23,000 per year; this matches the average graduate salary in 2021 of £21–25,000, as reported by www.graduate-jobs.com.

Rates from April 2022	First-year apprentice	Second-year apprentice or Higher Apprentice			
Age	16+	Under 18	18 to 20	21 to 22	23 and over
Minimum hourly wage	£4.81	£4.81	£6.83	£9.18	£9.50
Annual salary equivalent estimate	£8,800	£8,800	£12,500	£16,800	£17,400

Insight
When specialist practical skills count for more than academics

Did you know that a skilled bricklayer or carpenter who has trained as an apprentice can earn more than £50,000 a year? This is almost double the average graduate salary, which goes to show that specialist practical skills can, at times, lead to better pay than a degree.

In the case of tradespeople, the UK has had a construction skills shortage for some time, which means that construction bosses often struggle to fill roles. So much so, that research by the Federation of Master Builders in 2020 found that skilled bricklayers, carpenters and plasterers can earn an average of £53,200 a year – an amount that puts these individuals in the top 10% of earners in the UK.

This isn't to say, of course, that you should drop your studies and enrol onto a Level 2 bricklaying apprenticeship; if you're doing A levels, you already qualify for Higher Level apprenticeships. However, it shows how wrong the common perception is that apprenticeships only ever lead to low-paying work.

CHAPTER 5   DOING AN APPRENTICESHIP

Do Apprenticeships Prepare You for Work?

As apprenticeships are directly linked to a specific industry and employer, they are generally better than university at preparing you for work. There are some exceptions of course. If you wanted to pursue an academic field where you could advance theoretical knowledge, for example, then university would be the best preparation. But for most fields, especially the non-research kind, apprenticeships are an excellent introduction to the workplace.

A lot of apprentices and employers agree with this view, too. A government survey of apprentices and employers published in 2020 showed that nearly nine out of ten of them felt that their training had prepared them very (or fairly) well for their career plans; this is in contrast to just over half of graduates who feel that way. In the same survey, 85% of employers reported being satisfied with their apprenticeship programmes, and a similar percentage reported that apprentices developed skills that their organisations needed.

Apprenticeships succeed here because they train you directly in the field, doing real work with real industry professionals – something that university courses don't offer in most cases.

What are the Employment Prospects of Apprentices?

As soon as you start an apprenticeship you are employed, and you will remain so for at least 12 months (which is the minimum duration of any apprenticeship). So you could say that apprentices have a 100% employment rate, but that wouldn't be a fair comparison to the employment rate of graduates. Instead, we need to look at the percentage of apprentices who remain employed *after* completing their training.

Figures published by the UK government show that, since 2015, over 90% of apprentices have remained in work after their training. The statistics do vary across industries though. For example, 98 and 97% of apprentices in the construction and engineering industries respectively in 2018/19 were still in work after their training. In contrast, this figure was around 75% for arts and media apprentices. In both cases though, apprentices who complete their training are more likely to be in work than someone who has completed a degree.

This all sounds great, but there's a catch: It's one thing completing a high-quality apprenticeship; it's another matter securing that apprenticeship in the first place! The success rate of an apprenticeship application ranges from 5% to 40%, while that of securing a university place ranges from 10% to 90%, depending on course and institution.

Estimated range of applicant success rates for an apprenticeship versus a university place

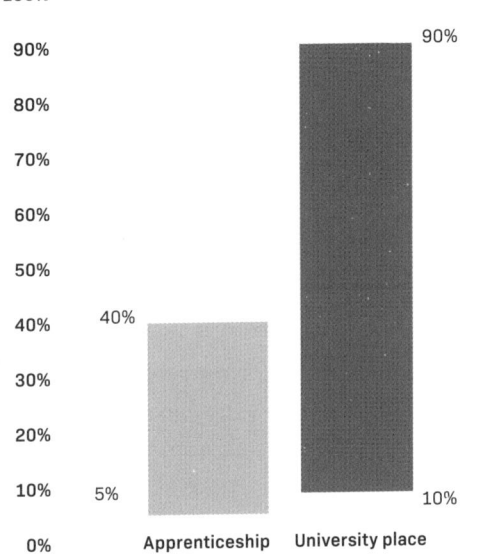

(Indicative estimates from a mix of 2020 UCAS data and 2016/17 Department of Education apprenticeship applicant data)

CHAPTER 5 DOING AN APPRENTICESHIP

Consider the example of BAE Systems, one of the UK's largest technology and engineering firms. While some businesses cut back on apprentice hires in 2020 due to the COVID-19 pandemic, BAE announced that it would press on with its recruitment drive to hire 800 apprentices. But – and this is a big but – they received over 9,000 applications! At that rate, only roughly 9% of applicants would succeed in getting a role. (In comparison, the success rate of getting into Oxford as an undergraduate – provided you have the necessary grades – is around 16% on average across all courses.) So although apprenticeships are more likely to secure future employment than a degree, the very best ones, such as the most lucrative ones at prestigious employers, are often harder to secure than university places.

> ### Insight
>
> #### The impact of the economy on apprenticeships
>
> Since apprenticeships are run by employers, the number of vacancies is especially sensitive to how well the economy is doing. At the height of the COVID-19 crisis in 2020, for example, around a third of employers believed that they would hire fewer apprentices in the coming year, according to a survey by educational charity the Sutton Trust. Almost one in three apprentices were furloughed in 2020 and almost one in five apprentices had their off-the-job training disrupted, as training providers stopped in-person teaching. However, eight in ten employers felt that training would resume as normal after lockdown restrictions ended.
>
> **So what can you do as an aspiring apprentice during an economic downturn?**
>
> First and foremost, you should have a back-up plan when applying for apprenticeships (more on that in the next Insight box).
>
> Secondly, consider some of the tips provided for graduates in the Insight box on page 57 of Chapter 4 on how to deal with a difficult job market, as these principles apply to apprentices too.

An Overview of Apprenticeships

All in all then, modern apprenticeships generally do a superb job of preparing people for a wide range of careers, and this is being increasingly recognised by employers. Well-known firms, such as the BBC, Nestlé, the Co-Op, Network Rail and BT, all take on apprentices across a range of departments these days. Although securing a good apprenticeship is generally more competitive than getting a place at university, it's a better way of learning real-world skills and getting paid while you're at it – so that you have no student debt! Furthermore, over 90% of apprentices remain in work after getting their qualification.

That said, apprenticeships work a lot better if you already have a strong idea of what you would like to do for work in the future. In fact, the candidates who secure high-quality apprenticeships tend to know what their goals are and can convincingly explain what their motivations and aspirations are when they are interviewed for an apprenticeship. They are also driven and determined to put in the effort needed to balance work and training.

All told then, how does an apprenticeship compare to a university placement? The answer will depend on your personal situation and a range of factors that we'll cover in Part Three. For now, the key takeaway is that apprenticeships do better than university at teaching practical skills and getting you into work.

However, apprenticeships aren't the only *alternative* to university after school. So in the next two chapters we'll look at alternative paths – in case neither university nor apprenticeships feel like quite the right thing for you.

Insight
Applying for apprenticeships

Applying for an apprenticeship is different to applying for a degree. Instead of using the UCAS system for university applications, apprentices apply directly to an employer or through a service such as *www.findapprenticeship.service.gov.uk*.

The process may include online and in-person tests, as well as multiple interview rounds. To keep on top of the process, be sure to keep the following tips in mind:

- **Application deadlines**. Unlike universities, employers have different application deadlines, so set a reminder for any apprenticeships you're interested in and make sure you don't miss important dates. Thankfully, many employers hire apprentices throughout the year so you'll have other options if you happen to miss a specific opportunity.

- **Online tests**. Some employers will ask you to complete an online test before you can progress to the next stage of your application. Depending on the job, these tests are usually a mix of maths, verbal and logic tests. So always research the apprenticeships that you're interested in to learn what type of tests are used and be sure to practise them as much as you can before taking them for real.

- **Assessment centres**. After the online application, you could be invited to complete certain assessments in person. Examples include giving a presentation, working in a group or doing a simulated task in a work environment. It can be tricky trying to prepare for these types of assessments, but consider speaking to your career advisors at school for help or practise with friends and relatives.

- **Interviews**. All apprenticeship programmes will have an interview, just like you would have for a regular job. So it's good to practise interview techniques before you get to this stage. Practise with your family, friends or a helpful teacher, as this can go a long way in calming any nerves you might have before an interview.

- **Unsuccessful applications**. Getting an apprenticeship is often so competitive that many apprentices have to make dozens of applications before they secure a role. So don't be disheartened if you aren't successful right away. Keep trying. And if you don't get one, don't be afraid to ask for feedback so that you can improve your next application.

- **Back-up plan**. Since securing the exact apprenticeship that you'd like isn't a guarantee, it's a good idea to have a back-up plan. Some candidates take a gap year and apply again in the following year but with additional work experience. Other candidates apply for an equivalent subject area at university. Others keep on applying for other related apprenticeships. There's no right or wrong here. It's just about keeping your options open about what might be right *for you*.

Chapter Recap

▶ Apprenticeships are effective at preparing you for the world of work and there are no tuition fees to pay. Instead, you get paid to train and work in your chosen field.

▶ A typical apprentice works for 30–40 hours a week and this time is split between on-the-job efforts (80% of the time) and off-the-job training and learning (20% of the time.)

▶ Higher Apprenticeships, which you can apply for if you have good A levels, are growing in popularity as they lead to qualifications that can result in similar or better outcomes than a degree.

▶ Over 90% of apprentices are in work shortly after their qualification, compared to around only 70% of graduates. However, these figures vary by subject area and industry.

▶ Apprenticeships are best suited to those who are clear about the career they wish to pursue and for whom practical work experience is important. Also, remember that the best apprenticeship vacancies can be more competitive than the best university courses.

6
WORKING YOUR WAY UP

Although university and apprenticeships are the most common paths to a variety of careers, they aren't the only way forward. If you have some ideas of what you'd like to do after school, but neither the thought of university or apprenticeships appeals to you, then it might be better to carve out your own path. In fact, in some professions it's possible to enter into an industry and effectively 'work your way up' from a junior role.

Let's take Eddie as an example. Eddie completed his A levels in Media Studies, Business and PE, and his grades were good enough for a university place. He briefly thought about following his sister – who was at university studying Leisure and Marketing – and liked the idea of a buzzing student social life and all the sports he could do while getting a degree. However, Eddie felt strongly that a workplace environment would be better for him. He had seen his dad working in the sports promotion business, and the idea of working with athletes felt exciting to him.

So instead of going to university or exploring apprenticeships, Eddie decided to find a way to go directly into work. He believed that doing that immediately, rather than spending three years on a degree, would give him more relevant real-life experience and a step up the ladder compared to graduates.

Though he had the option to work for his father, Eddie was driven to create opportunities for himself. He applied to over 20 different sports agencies and eventually landed a junior role as a Sponsorship Executive. This job matched his interests in sales and sports. He started on £12,000 a year, but this initial role helped him work his way up to becoming a major sports promoter.

This Eddie is none other than Eddie Hearn – one of the UK's top sports promoters. He has represented the likes of world champion boxer Anthony Joshua, and worked with YouTube stars KSI and Logan Paul on their celebrity boxing match in 2019.

Eddie is just one of many who have managed to break out to be hugely successful without a degree or apprenticeship. There are also plenty of stories about lesser-known 'everyday' people who have gone on to enjoy rewarding careers by 'working their way up' through the ranks of their chosen trade or industry.

How to Do Well On This Path

This route of 'working your way up' into a unique career isn't for everyone, as it will involve a significant amount of challenges and require a significant amount of self-determination. It also comes with less guidance compared to the more established routes of a university course or an apprenticeship. Still, it can be a very fulfilling path if you work hard and approach your development strategically. So here are some tips should you wish to pursue this route:

1. Find your skill and industry

First, you need to identify a skill that you believe you could be really good at – it might be a hobby that you'd like to develop more professionally, or an activity that you've shown promise in. If you aren't yet sure about which skill to pursue, that's fine. Some people discover it as they experiment with different ideas while at school; others only discover it after taking some time out to learn more about themselves (you'll find more about 'taking time out' in the next chapter).

Second, you need to research whether your desired skill has an industry that values it. This means that if you become good at that skill, you will also have the potential to be financially rewarded for it. Look for examples of people who've made a successful living from your chosen skill, since learning about these people's experiences can be inspirational.

2. Be disciplined

Once you've identified the skill and industry you'd like to pursue, you need a plan to guide your development. This could involve an online course, reading books, signing up to short courses at a college or university, as well as the real-world application of that skill. In this process you should aim to:

▶ **Have a timetable.** Since you may not have formal classes with this path, it's useful to create a timetable and carve out a certain number of hours a week, or a day, to develop your craft. If you've also got full-time or part-time work to contend with, try to use your weekends and evenings as wisely as possible to work on particular aspects of the skill that you want to develop.

▶ **Get regular feedback.** It's hard to learn anything well if you don't get feedback on your efforts. In formal education this is relatively easy thanks to grading systems and assessments. But outside of these areas there's often no clear way of checking your progress. One way of compensating for this is to find ways of getting regular feedback. For instance, if you take an online course, there might be opportunities to have your work assessed or marked. In creative sectors, you might be able to publish your work online and have other people review it. Alternatively, if you know anyone else who works in the area that you'd like to be in, you might want to ask them for valuable feedback (see also the next bullet).

▶ **Interact with experts.** One of the fastest ways to learn anything is to spend a lot of time with people who are more experienced than you. They can provide feedback on your work *and* guide your learning. If you struggle to find someone in real life, look for videos, books and podcasts created by experts. You can learn a lot from simply listening, watching and reading what experts have to say about their profession.

▶ **Find like-minded souls.** Without a university campus or apprenticeship programme you won't necessarily have a group of peers who are developing similar skills. But peer groups are important because you can support each other and share your experiences. As you develop a skill, it is therefore useful to seek out – either online or through local communities – groups of similarly motivated people.

3. Build a portfolio of achievements

If you choose to go straight into employment after your A levels, you won't get the widely recognised qualifications that you would get with a degree or apprenticeship. But that's not to say that you can't have something that showcases your talents. One way to evidence what you're capable of if you take this route is to build a 'portfolio' of achievements in a particular skill. You can then take this to potential employers (or customers) and demonstrate your ability to provide something of value to them.

Alternative Perspective

Alex Fefegha, Creative Technologist

Alex is an expert in design innovation, but his path was far from traditional. After school, he joined an apprenticeship programme but left it because he found the quality of training to be low. He then decided to apply to university instead, where he won a first-year tuition fee scholarship because of his strong A level grades.

However, Alex's university course ended up being a poor fit for him, so he decided to move away from that path as well. Meanwhile, he had independently developed his skills in design innovation and had started a consulting business with a friend. Over the years, they won business contracts with the NHS, the BBC and Uber. The quality of this experience meant that when Alex decided to reconsider university, he was able to secure a place on a master's programme without an undergraduate degree.

Alex went on to gain a distinction in his master's degree, but his motivation was different from most graduates. Here's how he recalls his journey:

> 'The master's for me was never about the degree... there's a difference between a bachelor's degree and a master's degree. A bachelor's is very much focussed on learning the basics of your chosen subject, whereas a master's is very much about developing independent thinking around a particular research topic that you're interested in. And the latter is what I needed.
>
> '[Today] nobody is asking me about my degree. People ask me about my ability to solve a problem. That's what people are interested in: "What's your working process? How do you think?" So my master's [was] a place for me to just build a way to think... And that's why I always say to people, if we can redefine our relationship with education, it will be more beneficial for people. If we change the relationship with university from looking for a job to the personal development of your interest, I'm guessing [many] people would choose a different degree from what they studied.'

Below are a few helpful ways to build portfolios across a range of careers that don't need university degrees or other formal qualifications. If they don't apply to what *you* would like to do, they will at least give you some ideas about how to start building a portfolio in your own area:

- **Software engineer:** Build a portfolio of apps that you've worked on and share them with others on the code-hosting platform GitHub.com.
- **Writer:** Start a blog or newsletter and publish content regularly over a meaningful period of time (for example, six months to a year). Once you have an archive of work, you can pitch for writing opportunities with various publications by sharing your 'online writing' portfolio.
- **Actor:** Work on short films with local talent. This allows you to accumulate material that showcases your talent, which you can then share with casting directors.

Some Specific Career Insights

On pages 89–92 is a sample of jobs in various industries that you may or may not have considered. What's interesting about these examples is that you might have expected that a degree or other formal qualification would be necessary for them, but as you'll see, there are often alternative pathways.

The examples obviously only touch the tip of the iceberg in terms of the wide range of job options that are out there, but UCAS have a fantastic resource for discovering more careers at: *www.ucas.com/careers-advice*.

Independent Financial Adviser

What does an independent financial adviser do?

Independent financial advisers – also sometimes known as 'IFAs'– help people to manage and invest their finances appropriately. This includes help with mortgages, pensions and investments in businesses, property or other areas that preserve and build wealth. IFAs must provide advice that is independent and best-suited to a client, and their profession is regulated by the UK's Financial Conduct Authority.

The IFA profession is suitable for anyone that enjoys working with people, staying in the know about financial products and services, and giving advice.

How do you become an IFA

A business degree or apprenticeship can be beneficial to become an IFA. However, many IFAs build careers in the industry without having taken either of these routes. One alternative path is to start as a 'paraplanner' – a non-client-facing junior person who supports a more qualified financial adviser by helping with research and compliance. You could then pursue a Diploma in Regulated Financial Planning, which would help you to secure more senior roles. (Some firms support their paraplanners by paying for these qualifications.)

If you're interested in pursuing a career in this area, it's worth checking out the websites of the Chartered Banker Institute, the Chartered Insurance Institute and the London Institute of Banking and Finance.

Interior Designer

What does an interior designer do?

Interior designers create specific, coordinated styles for homes, commercial spaces and other buildings. They assess property, produce detailed designs and choose things like suitable upholstery, wallpaper, furniture and decorative objects for each project. This role is suitable for anyone that enjoys working with properties in a creative way.

How do you become an interior designer?

The preferred route to becoming an interior designer is to take a degree or HND/HNC in interior design, interior architecture or spatial design. Many applicants also complete a Foundation Diploma in Art and Design before applying for higher education.

However, entrance in the absence of formal qualifications is possible for someone with relevant experience, enthusiasm and an exceptional portfolio. Regardless of qualifications held, prior voluntary or part-time work experience is usually imperative to securing full-time employment in this area. Placements will help you to become familiar with key industry tools (such as computer design software) while building up your portfolio of work.

Contact details for interior designers when looking for work placements can be found through the British Institute of Interior Design and the Chartered Society of Designers. Competition is fierce, so networking and sending applications even if a job isn't advertised is recommended.

CHAPTER 6 WORKING YOUR WAY UP

Film and TV Producer

What does a film and TV producer do?

Producers in the film industry are the businesspeople of a project. They 'project manage' a production, work out how much funding is required for a film or TV show, allocate resources, recruit talent and, in the early days of a project, might even provide creative ideas on a script. This role requires strong communication, organisation and people skills. The job is suited to people who are good at juggling different hats and have a passion for media and business.

How do you become a film and TV producer?

Film and TV producers do a little bit of everything on a project, so there's no one way of entering the profession. Nor are there any specific qualifications required. Most people work their way up by working on small independent projects, pursuing internships or working as assistants to experienced staff.

It's also possible to enrol on short courses that can help you to network and find a job in the industry. For instance, in 2021, if you were aged 18, you could apply for a free course through the National Film and Television School to get experience as a production assistant. This course included both theoretical and practical learning.

The creative industries are generally tough to crack as there's so much demand to work within them, so you'll need to be smart about networking and finding a way to get experience. Organisations such as the National Film and Television School and ScreenSkills can be useful places to start.

Editorial Assistant

What does an editorial assistant do?

Editorial assistants support more senior staff in the publishing industry with editorial and administrative tasks. This includes proofreading documents, liaising with authors on project timelines, collecting and helping review new book projects, and offering a variety of support, from the conception of a project through to completion.

Editorial assistants work to tight deadlines and often have multiple projects on at the same time. This means they need to be well-organised and good at time management. IT skills are also favourable since editorial assistants work with a variety of specialist software, such as Adobe InDesign.

This role is suitable for people who are interested in the publishing industry and have a good eye for written content and how it's presented.

How do you become an editorial assistant?

It's possible to enter the industry without a degree. For example, one of the top publishers in the industry, Penguin Random House, introduced a traineeship in 2015 called 'The Scheme', which offered paid internships to people without degrees or experience in the industry. Since 2021, there has been a particular focus on opening up the publishing industry to ethnic minorities and people from a low socio-economic background. You can learn more at *www.the-scheme.co.uk*.

Another way to work your way up as an editorial assistant is to start as a general assistant at a publishing firm and seek in-house training and promotion. You may find it useful to undertake a proofreading or editing course offered by The Publishing Training Centre, for example. The Society of Young Publishers also holds networking events throughout the UK that are worth exploring as they can help you to meet key industry contacts.

An Overview of Working Your Way Up

It's possible to go straight from school into the workplace if the area of work that you're interested in doesn't need a specific degree or professional apprenticeship. This route can be exciting, creative and, for some, hugely successful. Remember, though, that it will demand a lot from you, including maturity, patience, hard work, motivation and determination – to name but a few of the qualities required.

If you are, however, a self-starter, with a strong sense of your talents, and you are ready to take a structured and disciplined approach to becoming skilled in something that you are passionate about, then there's no reason why you can't do just as well as any graduate or apprentice in the long term.

Chapter Recap

▶ It might seem like there are only two respected choices after school – going to university or doing an apprenticeship – but you can also go straight to the workplace at the age of 18 and work your way up.

▶ Since this path is outside of the more established training paths, it requires more personal discipline. You're therefore likely to have to make greater efforts in mastering a craft that's useful and is likely to lead to employment.

▶ Self-starters who take this route are usually good with people, know their talents and are willing to network their way to an internship or junior role that can act as a springboard to their dream job.

7
TAKING TIME OUT TO THINK

Aspiring drama school students might have heard of the award-winning playwright and screenwriter Anya Reiss. Her plays have been staged at West End theatres, and she's credited as a writer on 27 episodes of the BBC's long-running soap *EastEnders*.

Anya discovered her passion for writing in her early teens after reluctantly attending a writing course that her mum had suggested for the holidays. Although Anya considered going to university – and had half-heartedly applied to study English Literature at Cambridge University – she ended up taking a gap year instead. Her plan was to write two plays in that time, before returning to her decision of whether to go to university or not.

Part way into her gap year, and after reflecting on her future, Anya chose to abandon the university route. She didn't like the idea of taking an academic path and felt ready to focus entirely on the theatre industry. In addition, her first play had already been selected to be shown at the Royal Court Theatre – quite an achievement! This meant that not opting for the traditional path wasn't as risky, since by the time her decision came round she had already made great strides in the theatre industry.

Not everyone can be as lucky as Anya. However, the 'time out' that she gave herself in the form of a gap year – in order to make her decision about what to do next – is a great example of how to give yourself some thinking space after school if you can afford to do so.

In this brief chapter we'll look at how taking time out like this can be used effectively to set yourself up for success.

When to Consider Taking Time Out

If by the end of this book you still aren't sure about what you'd like to do after school, it might be worth considering taking a little time out from your focus on education and training through what is known as a 'gap year' (or a shorter time if required). This gives you space to further reflect on your options, and consider, or experiment with, other possible training routes – at the same time as getting a little more life experience under your belt.

Before venturing out though, remember that, although in the UK you can leave school after age 16, in England there's another region-specific requirement: you have to continue with some form of recognised education or training, such as sixth form, college, apprenticeships, or part-time work alongside part-time education, until you're 18.

You'll also need to consider whether you'd like to stay at home or travel during your time out, and, either way, whether your family are able to support you, or whether you'll need to secure at least part-time or temporary work to fund any activities you decide to pursue in the year. (Around eight in ten students work at some point during their gap year.)

> **Insight**
>
> **Taking time out, but applying to university now**
>
> Some students apply to university but request to defer their entry to a course by a year. This allows them time to try and explore other things with the security of already having a university place. If this is an option that you're interested in, you'll need to check with the specific university and course as to whether it is something that they offer.
>
> This deferral option isn't possible with apprenticeships. However, as mentioned earlier, a bonus of apprenticeships is that employers recruit apprentices *throughout* the year, which means that you don't have to worry about only being able to apply at a certain time, as is the case with university (September to January). This means that if you do take 'time out' before applying for an apprenticeship, you could use it for work experience that helps you to test out an area of interest before you fully commit to it via the apprenticeship.

The Benefits of Taking Time Out

There are no rules on how to take time out. A gap year, for instance, can take many forms; it's totally up to you. But it helps to have a plan so that you can make the most of the experience without the time drifting by with nothing to show for it. Think about what you would like to have achieved in a year or so's time so that you can work towards these things.

Some of the benefits of time out, such as a gap year, include:

- ▶ **Time to think.** Spending a year out of education without the pressure of having to figure things out right away can be invaluable if you can afford to do it. It is often a particularly welcome relief if you feel pressured by UCAS deadlines and the expectations of others. And given that taking a break in this way isn't unusual these days, it doesn't come with any stigma – you just have to make the gap year constructive.

▶ **Personal development.** Some people choose to spend a year abroad volunteering, others choose to work part-time or full-time near home, and some choose to build new skills such as learning a foreign language or other expertise. Whatever you choose to do, the best gap years involve efforts of personal development. If you do this, you'll find that your prospects of getting a university place, apprenticeship, or any other form of training placement or a job are higher. You'll also know yourself better, including which path of training or education is likely to be best for you.

▶ **Earnings with learnings.** A gap year can also be used to earn and save money that will provide a financial cushion for whatever educational path you take later. Naturally, getting real work experience also enhances your CV and professional network, both of which are important, no matter what route you choose after school.

Practical Resources for a Gap Year

There are several organisations that help students make the most of their gap years. Some of these charge fees, so if you opt for this route, keep an eye out for costs that you might have to cover with earnings from part-time work, savings or family support. In addition, the COVID-19 pandemic led to travel restrictions which may or may not continue, so be sure to consider local opportunities, as well as foreign ones.

Here's a list of some reputable places where you can look for more information:

▶ **UCAS gap year ideas.** This is an excellent section on gap year ideas that anyone can benefit from: *www.ucas.*

> ## Insight
> ### Keeping your brain sharp during a gap year
>
> If there's a chance you might want to go to university after a gap year, it's important to keep academically active where possible. For example, in STEM subjects (science, technology, engineering and maths), as in many others, it's easy to forget advanced knowledge if it isn't routinely practised. So check the websites of any specific university courses that interest you and see if they recommend anything in particular in terms of prep for applying.
>
> You can also take advantage of online courses or textbooks that can help you stay sharp, such as:
>
> - *www.edx.org*
> - *www.khanacademy.org*
> - *www.futurelearn.com*

com/alternatives/gap-year/gap-years-ideas-and-things-think-about.

▶ **Gap year safety information.** The UK government has a handy guide on how to stay safe should you choose to go abroad: *www.gov.uk/guidance/safer-adventure-travel-and-volunteering-overseas.*

▶ **Best Gap Year.** This website provides information on gap year programmes, paid work experience and teaching opportunities abroad, as well as travel adventures across the world: *www.bestgapyear.co.uk.*

▶ **Camp America.** This organisation provides the opportunity to live and work at a summer camp in the USA for a number of weeks: *www.campamerica.co.uk.* You can support the camp in many ways, including kitchen work, teaching children, administrative tasks and more.

▶ **Gapforce.** This company offers adventure travel, marine conservation, wildlife conservation, and outdoor courses for students of all types. For example, you can qualify as a dive instructor over ten weeks, learn expedition medicine, or build your bushcraft and survival skills on a five-day course. The fees for these courses range from £350 for a one-week programme in the UK to £2,500 or more for a month-long trip in South America for instance: *gapforce.org*.

An Overview of Taking Time Out

Taking a year out can be a positive and productive experience, and is unlikely to hold you back in terms of career progression if you plan it well and invest in developing yourself.

If, however, you were to spend time out doing very little to develop your skills and grow as a person, you might find that you end up lagging behind at university or on other training schemes. So if you do decide on this option, be sure to get a plan of learning and personal growth together from the get-go, so that you know what you're aiming for.

Chapter Recap

▶ When faced with a big decision, you don't always have to choose right away. You can, if your situation allows it, take time out to think and allow yourself a little more space to consider what's best.

▶ One way to give yourself time with the decision of what to do after school is to consider a gap year (or a shorter period if necessary). You might choose to do part-time work, volunteer or take up short courses to develop yourself within this time.

▶ Some gap year students still apply for university but defer it by a year. While apprenticeship applicants don't have this option, they can look for work-experience opportunities to test the waters in an industry before they commit to it.

▶ There's no stigma to taking time out to think; and it doesn't necessarily close any doors. However, it only works well if you plan the time carefully and spend it productively.

Part Two: Conclusion

By now, you will have realised that there are no easy or 'ideal' one-size-fits-all choices when it comes to what to do after school. University is a well-established and respected route but it doesn't always prepare you well for the world of work. Apprenticeships do a better job of preparing you for the real world (plus you get paid to learn rather than having to pay to learn!), but the best ones can be more competitive than getting into university. In addition, it's possible to do well after school with alternative approaches, such as working your way up in a career without a degree or apprenticeship. However, in this instance you have to be okay with taking a more risky, independent route.

Each path has its pros and cons, so you have to think about your individual case and compare each path in more than one way. In Part Three we will do exactly that, by considering and comparing the two most established paths in more detail: university and apprenticeships.

PART THREE

HOW TO DECIDE: THE FIVE KEY FACTORS

In trying to choose what route to take when you leave school, you might well be asking yourself questions like: Which path will lead to more career options? Which option suits the way I learn? What's the real price tag and financial reward of each path anyway? And should I also consider what's on offer socially with each option? This part of the book will guide you through five key factors that address these questions in the context of choosing between the two most established paths of university and apprenticeships. Note, however, that even though we are looking at just university and apprenticeships within this section – in order to let you see a direct comparison process in action – you can use the same train of analytical thinking with other options, too. You would do this by comparing two different paths against each other across the factors we will discuss in the following chapters.

8
YOUR CAREER OPTIONS

People often think that if you have a university degree you'll also have more career options to pick from, and that having more options is always a good thing. Take someone who studies an arts subject at university – say English Literature. This person is likely to be eligible for a wide range of jobs after uni that might appeal to them – everything from journalist and editor to management consultant and marketing executive. This is because even though many employers ask for a degree, they often don't mind what subject that degree is in.

Now, compare that with someone who does a Nursery Manager apprenticeship, for example. Most people might think that this apprentice has fewer career options because their specialist training ties them to a specific field, and that this leaves them worse off.

However, in this chapter we'll see that this kind of thinking isn't entirely accurate. A degree may indeed present more career options – and this can be helpful – but there are situations where narrowing your options earlier on can give you an advantage. So let's look a little closer at this and see how it might affect your decision.

The Pros and Cons of Increasing your Options

When more is good
A path that keeps the door open for multiple career options can be very appealing, since it removes the pressure to figure things out straight away. It also means you can change direction more easily in the future if you want to.

Having options is also useful in times of economic uncertainty. When the wider economy isn't doing so well, for example, people sometimes have to consider alternative careers if jobs in their preferred industry dry up. In those situations, people with a broader education often have more flexibility.

Ultimately, having more options, also called 'optionality', provides some protection from an uncertain future – whether that's uncertainty in what you'd like to do after school or uncertainty with what's happening in the wider economy. But optionality also has limitations that are not always obvious…

When less is better
If all your education and career choices are based on keeping the widest number of options open, you're likely to run into a number of issues.

First, when you try to keep lots of career doors open, you risk spreading yourself too thin. In other words, you risk not being able to give enough focussed time, energy and effort to any one specialist option, as you're stretching yourself in so many different directions.

CHAPTER 8 YOUR CAREER OPTIONS

> **Alternative Perspective**
>
> ## Seyed Boutorabi, First Officer at Emirates Airlines
>
> Seyed is a First Officer at Emirates Airlines. He decided to specialise early on because he saw no benefit in delaying his career journey just to get more options. He knew what he wanted to do for work, and he decided to pursue it straight after sixth form:
>
> *'I went to pilot school when I was 18, and I always knew from a young age that I wanted to be a pilot. In the pilot profession, time and age can be an important factor. I had the option to study Aeronautical Engineering at Coventry Uni, but I wanted to start training right away, and in the airline industry if you start early that can be a good thing. That's because if you start training at 18, you can qualify in your early 20s and airlines like hiring new pilots young, so they can mould them to their airline practices, which can be harder if you qualify much later. Also, if you qualify in your 20s, you can potentially fly for 45 years until retirement, while someone who went to uni first and then qualifies in their 30s may miss out on ten years of flying.'*

Consider a graduate of International Relations, for example. Even though they'll no doubt have a good, *broad* education, an employer recruiting for an entry-level position in, let's say, HR (human resources), may prefer an apprentice or graduate who has specialised in that field already.

Plentiful options are also less useful for people who are already confident about what they want to do after school. So if you are one of these people, it might well be better to get an immediate head-start by training in your *specific* area of interest, rather than spending years widening your career options with a generalist education.

Another potential issue with making choices just to maximise career options is that it could turn into a habit of avoiding commitment – a bit like 'kicking the can down the road'. Here's a tweet from a successful technology entrepreneur and investor that nicely summarises what you *shouldn't* do in this respect:

Erik Torenberg ✓
@eriktorenberg

We're obsessed w/ optionality:

"I don't know what I'm gonna do w/ my life so I'm gonna get a degree"

"I don't know what to do w/ this degree so I'm gonna get a grad degree"

"I don't know what to do w/ grad degree so I'm gonna get consulting job to figure out what job I want."

11:37 PM · Jan 8, 2019 · Twitter Web Client

Erik Torenberg, Partner at Village Global
(an Economics and English Literature graduate)

So, although having more options has its benefits, we shouldn't let this stop us from trying to bravely commit to a more focussed choice that will ultimately benefit us and our personal development. Think back to how you chose your A levels. If university was something you were thinking about, did you make your A level choices based only on the goal of having the broadest choice of university courses open to you? Or did you pick subjects in areas that you were genuinely interested in, even if it narrowed what you could do after school?

Now that we know the pros and cons of aiming to maximise your options, let's look at how optionality varies between university and apprenticeships, and what this means for your decision on whether to go to university or take an alternative route.

CHAPTER 8   YOUR CAREER OPTIONS

What Choices can University Give You?

University can lead to a wide pool of career options, depending on what subject you get your degree in. For example, a Classics or Geography graduate might be able to secure a wide variety of roles, from digital marketer to political risk analyst. A Transport Planning apprentice or Childcare trainee, on the other hand, would have a slimmer option pool due to their specialist training.

One of the reasons for this difference is that many employers believe that a university education provides a good level of general life skills, such as research ability, independent learning and critical thinking, which are transferable to many other work areas.

However, it seems to me that the optionality advantage of a degree is sometimes oversold. Although research suggests that around a third of graduates enter roles that require a specific degree (meaning that there should be a two-thirds majority who go into jobs that *don't* need a specialist degree), this varies significantly by sector. For example, around half of business and management jobs don't require employees with a specific degree subject, but over 90% of roles in sciences do. This is, of course, something that you'd expect: a technical role in a pharmaceutical research company is unlikely to be a fit for, say, a language graduate compared to someone with a relevant sciences degree; whereas a language graduate could, in theory, be a good fit for a role in business management if that's where their interests lie.

A final point here takes us back to our example of the Classics and Geography graduates versus the Transport Planning and Childcare apprentices. The range of career options that these graduates have, whether digital marketing, political risk analysis or whatever else, are irrelevant to the specialist apprentice if the

Insight
How police career paths have changed

The training requirements for careers are always changing. For example, many large companies used to ask for degrees in their professional career programmes – today, many don't.

Changes can also happen in the other direction. For example, before 2020, you didn't need a degree to be a police officer in England and Wales. However, the College of Policing have since made changes to their requirements, meaning that all police officers now have to be educated to degree level. Fortunately, there are a variety of entry routes to help with this:

1. **Graduate Entry (Any Degree)** Graduates from any discipline can join the police force, but there's further learning and training that then happens both on- and off-the-job, which leads to a graduate diploma in Professional Policing and normally takes two years.
2. **Police Constable Degree Apprenticeship (a 'PCDA')** This is typically a three-year programme, where you start as a constable and develop with on- and off-the-job learning. This apprenticeship leads to a degree in Professional Policing Practice. You need at least two A levels to be eligible.
3. **Pre-Join Degree in Professional Policing** This is a specialist degree that focusses on the academic knowledge of policing. It might be ideal for people who are interested in how justice and policing work in society, but perhaps aren't sure if they specifically want to work as a constable. This degree could be *beneficial* if applying to be a constable, but it wouldn't guarantee a job. All recruits still have to meet a police force's requirements, and holders of the degree must apply for police roles within five years of graduation. Furthermore, only a few universities offer this degree, so if you're interested, check the College of Policing website for more details (*www.college.police.uk/career-learning/joining-new-pc/universities-offering-professional-policing-degree*).

You can see from just this one example how important it is to keep an eye on how training requirements are changing for different areas of work and different roles.

apprentice has no interest in industries other than the one that they've chosen to focus on.

In other words, having lots of options is pointless if you're never going to use them. You might as well benefit instead from additional years of work experience by heading straight to a trainee position in your industry of choice after school.

In effect, the optionality that you get by pursuing a broad degree at university is therefore only worthwhile if you aren't sure about the career that you'd like to pursue. And in that case, established

> ## **Graduate Perspective**
>
> ### Anthony Spencer, Sports Science graduate (now a Project Management Consultant)
>
> We first met Anthony, a Sports Science graduate, in Chapter 4. He wasn't always sure about what he wanted to do after university, but he has learned that transferable skills in any subject can still get you far. He says:
>
> > 'I chose university, as with the qualifications I had at the time there weren't any jobs which I was really drawn to. At that point, I had been doing Sport Science at college [but] I wasn't really interested in coaching. I did, however, like the idea of being somewhat of a scientist. So, with no clear paths deviating from education, I decided to look at universities. I found one with great facilities and where I really felt I would enjoy the culture. I figured I would be there for three years, so I wanted to like where I would be studying.
> >
> > 'Truthfully though, it's very likely the person you are in your teens – when you are trying to make this decision – will be motivated by things vastly different from those of the person you become in your late 20s, 30s and so on. So, never expect that you are going to know 100%, but don't let that stress you out, transferable skills are king.'

Insight
Broad versus specialised degree subjects

University offers many degrees that can be used to secure jobs in a wide variety of areas. For example, one employment survey (see chart below) found that although 11% of Sociology graduates entered specialised roles for their degree, this meant that almost 90% of them went into work that wasn't closely related to their studies. Another case example from the same survey was Maths graduates – while 24% of them went into specialised maths fields, this meant that more than three-quarters of the group went into other areas.

However, universities also offer a lot of courses these days that are more vocational (i.e. subject areas that are more linked to a specific job), such as Dentistry, Nursing, Pharmacy, Architecture, Civil Engineering, Software Engineering and Accounting – as can also be seen in the chart below.

According to further data from the Higher Education Funding Council for England (now known as the Office for Students), these kinds of specialist degrees often lead to greater employment prospects (and higher pay) than the more generalist ones. (Similar results would be expected for specialised apprenticeship routes.)

Percentage of graduates in specialist jobs related to their degree

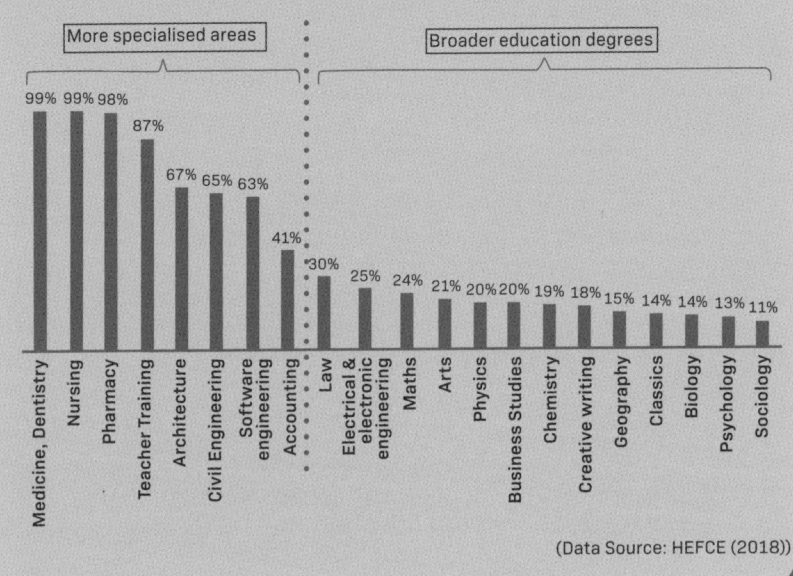

(Data Source: HEFCE (2018))

disciplines like Maths, Sciences, Engineering, Business and Languages, are useful for opening a range of career doors. However, if you choose university just to delay committing to a specific area of work that you might be interested in, you risk losing out on years of work experience that could propel your career forward sooner.

Apprenticeships and Specialism

Apprenticeships focus on a specific type of work. This means that they tend not to offer as broad a range of career options as degrees can provide. For example, a Foreign Exchange Broker apprentice would be well suited to working in the foreign exchange industry and perhaps even in other areas of finance. However, if they attempted to switch to a completely different area of work, say project management or logistics, they might find it hard to compete against a graduate with a broader university education. As we saw earlier, this is because some employers believe university does a good job of developing a range of intellectual skills that you can then transfer and use to your advantage in lots of different settings.

That said, the ability of apprenticeships to develop these same kind of transferable skills is often underappreciated. Despite the perception of over-specialism, there are hundreds of apprenticeships across Engineering, Science, Technology, Business and more that can make your future just as flexible as a graduate.

Certainly, there are some very specialist areas – such as within Construction and Agriculture – where most of what you learn is unlikely to open doors in *completely* different industries. But even then, the advantage of an apprenticeship is that you get to learn other non-technical skills that are harder to learn in a class or with a textbook. These include things like how to work with people from different age groups and cultures, how to find a solution to a customer's problem, how the commercial and business worlds work in real life, and how to adapt rapidly to changing environments. These are all transferable 'soft' skills that you're more likely to get with an apprenticeship than with a degree.

> ## Insight
> ### Reflecting on your interests and options
>
> - **'I'm not sure about the career I want'**
>
> If you aren't sure about careers yet, it could be worth reflecting on whether you enjoy studying mostly with facts and figures or whether you're more drawn to the fluidity of the arts and humanities.
>
> If you're in the first group, a technical degree at university, such as economics, maths, sciences, technology or engineering, could be a good fit.
>
> If you're in the second group, you might want to consider a less technical but equally well-established subject area, such as literature, languages, history, psychology or business.
>
> Any of these subjects, whether technical or less so, are likely to set you up well for plenty of career choices when you graduate.
>
> - **'I'm sure about the career I want'**
>
> If you're confident that you know exactly what you'd like to do for a living, look for a path that will get you there in the most effective way. Just remember that some jobs come without options (for example, doctors have to do a medical degree), while other jobs offer some flexibility (for example, you need a degree-level education to work as a police constable, but there are a range of options to obtain this – see the box on page 110).
>
> It's therefore important to research your desired industry, and role, carefully – so that you know what's required to get into it.

CHAPTER 8 YOUR CAREER OPTIONS

So, although some apprenticeship programmes might narrow what you can do after you qualify, there are many courses that will provide you with skills that are useful across a variety of workplaces.

Establishing the Right Choice for You – based on Career Options

If you don't yet know what area of work you'd like to pursue after school, a broad education at university could be a good bet, as it gives you time to learn more about yourself while also developing transferable intellectual skills.

On the other hand, if you have clarity about your dream job, you might be better off taking the path that gets you to your career goals most effectively. That could mean a more specialised degree, an apprenticeship or perhaps some other route, as we saw with the pilot example on page 107.

Chapter Recap

▶ This chapter has focussed on the importance of understanding the range of careers that you will have access to depending on which route you choose to take after school; this can also be thought of as 'optionality'.

▶ A broad education at university can maximise your optionality, and is especially suitable if you aren't sure about what you'd like to do for work in the future.

▶ However, if you know what you want to do after school, optionality isn't as important. This is because you can start focussing on your career goals right away rather than spread yourself thin by trying to keep lots of career doors open.

9
YOUR LEARNING PREFERENCES

It's likely that by the age of three, you had mastered how to manipulate some 40 different speech sounds (called phonemes) in order to be able to utter hundreds of different words. This means that, before you ever started to learn about the English language in a more formal, structured way at school, you had learned all the basics through everyday listening, trial and error, and practical application.

Learning a new language is just one of many examples that showcase how learning works best: a combination of practice and theory.

Let's face it. On the whole, theory without practice is no good, but neither is practice without theory. In other words, if you only read about a language at school and didn't speak it, you'd struggle to pick it up. And if you only spoke it and never studied its theoretical elements, you would find it hard to appreciate and make sense of its nuances.

> **Insight**
>
> **Learning styles versus learning preferences**
>
> There's a theory that different people learn better through different learning styles, such as:
>
> - Visual learning – looking at things like videos and diagrams
> - Audio learning – listening to things like lectures and podcasts
> - Physical ('kinaesthetic') learning – doing things in a 'hands-on' way
>
> Although many people subscribe to this theory, my view is that people are too dynamic and flexible to be boxed into such exclusive categories – whether visual, audio or physical. Instead, we all learn best via a *mix* of styles.
>
> That said, I do think that we all have learning *preferences*. So you might, for example, *prefer* visual learning over audio learning, or audio learning over physical learning. And your learning *preferences* might extend more broadly than this to academic/theoretical learning over practical/hands-on learning, or vice versa.
>
> Whatever your preference, it doesn't mean that using just one approach in isolation will be the best thing for you. Because, although you might *prefer* one method over another, your progress may suffer if you stick to just one technique. Here's how educational psychologist Paul Kirschner makes this point, using a food-preference analogy:
>
> > *'... while most people prefer sweet, salty and/or fatty foods, I think we can all agree that this is not the most effective diet to follow, except if the goal is to become unhealthy and overweight.'*
>
> The point here is that it's good to get to *know* your preferences – whether for food flavours or for approaches to learning – and that it's also then good to ensure that you are exposed through your choices to a suitable balance of approaches.

Without a doubt, learning is most effective when theoretical and practical learning come together. But, as you now know, university degrees and apprenticeships tend to give different weights to these two approaches to learning – with university being more theoretical and academic, and apprenticeships being more practical and hands-on.

Given that we each tend to have personal preferences in terms of how we best learn, it's really important to make sure you know your own learning preferences in order to better gauge what the next best steps might be for you after school.

In this chapter we'll explore how you can identify where you sit on the learning preference spectrum of 'academic' versus 'practical' – which should reveal which route of further education you're more likely to appreciate. But first, let's cover a basic question: why should we care about learning in the first place?

The Power of Learning: A Lifelong Affair

Why bother with school? What's the point of education anyway?

Thoughts like this are more common than people like to admit, and often crop up in boring late afternoon classes and the like. In these moments, education can feel like a real chore – as if you're just going through the motions of what you 'have' to do to 'get a good job' and 'have a good future'.

But is there more to learning than just doing it for the sake of qualifications and jobs? It took me years to appreciate this but yes, there really is so much more to learning than just this. Ultimately, the process of learning equips you with the know-how to navigate the world intelligently. And, regardless of whether this knowledge is achieved inside or outside of the classroom, being 'educated' gives you the raw materials you need to access opportunities that you wouldn't otherwise be able to. (You may also be surprised by the delight you get from learning something really well, especially when it's hard at first.)

Think back to the language example we had earlier. If you hadn't learned to speak and understand English, you'd be missing out on a lot right now – and not just the vital aspects of life, such as being able to communicate your needs, but also fun things, like the joy of watching a film or the pleasure of reading a gripping novel – activities that would become even more plentiful if you knew multiple languages.

Simply put, life is richer when you know how to learn well and you appreciate the value of knowledge. So learning (and education in general) is always a worthwhile investment.

Pairing Academic and Practical Learning

We've already seen through the example of language that the best way to learn is to marry academic and practical methods. But let's now consider another example to further illustrate the point.

If you wanted to become a pilot, you wouldn't spend all your time training in a classroom, as important as that may be. You'd also spend lots of hours in a flight simulator and eventually, in a real aircraft. It goes without saying, of course, that you need the academic 'classroom' element to teach you the theoretical knowledge, such as the principles of flight and aerodynamics. But you *also* need the real-world practice to get the experience of dealing with a range of unexpected situations among other things. As such, it would be the *combination* of the theory and practice that would lead you to pass your exams and become a good pilot.

This is how learning works best in all other areas of life, too: effective learners always aim to get a balanced diet of intellectual scholarship and real-world know-how.

Learning Approaches at University versus in Apprenticeships

The mix of theory and practice is very different at university and in apprenticeships. University courses generally spend more time on academic learning while apprenticeships spend more time on practical learning and applied knowledge. The figure below, based on the 20/80% split of theory and practice introduced in Chapter 5, broadly illustrates the mix of learning approaches that exists within each of these two routes.

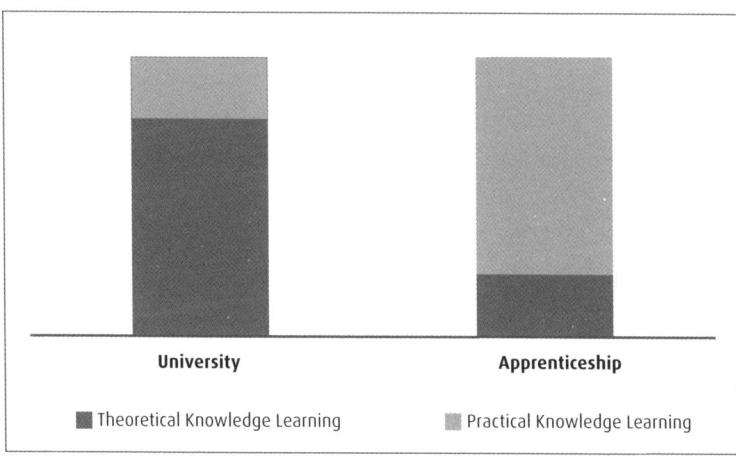

Ideally, your choice of what to do after school will suit your learning preference, because this can inspire and motivate you to get the most out of your chosen path. So if you enjoy practical, hands-on guidance and 'doing', an apprenticeship could be a worthwhile choice. On other hand, if you prefer to learn by reading and learning theory, you might be better off at university. Both routes can lead to good outcomes, but before you make your final choice it's important to know the strengths and weaknesses of each learning approach.

University and the Academic Path

Universities are historically known for their focus on academic rather than vocational subjects. This includes subjects with a broad reach such as philosophy, history, maths and science, as opposed to hands-on subjects where learning is directly linked to a specific job. Although the focus of degree subjects has changed over the years – for example, there are now degrees in more vocational subjects such as nursing, landscape design and teacher training – *most* learning at university is still largely academic and conceptual.

This focus on academics has both pros and cons. University is a fantastic place for scholarship. You get access to knowledgeable professors who do lots of research in their fields; and you learn how to think deeply, how to analyse things critically, and how to research the academic realm for the best ideas that can be applied in practice once you graduate.

People who want to pursue an academic career, such as becoming a theoretical physicist or professor of biology, are likely to feel 'at home' at university; the nature of these careers is that they require long periods of academic study before the practical work of scientific research can begin.

But, although university works well for those who are academically inclined, it doesn't tend to offer many opportunities to *apply* what

> # Graduate Perspective
>
> ## Christopher Nolan, English Graduate (now a Film Director)
>
> Christopher Nolan is a well-known movie director (if you haven't watched any of his films, start with *The Dark Knight*!), who studied English literature at university, not film-making. His practical learning of how films work happened independently, yet he still found value in the university experience. In an interview for the *Daily Telegraph*, which was conducted as a conversation with his ex-English professor (someone who also taught an optional film module), Nolan recounted the value he got from university:
>
> > 'I started making films when I was about 7, and I figured out I wanted to be a film director when I was 11 or 12. My dad was very encouraging but pointed out that you might want to get a degree in something unrelated to what you want to do because it gives a different take on things. And certainly, doing English literature was great. Being forced to think more about how we read books, [and] analyse books, was very useful. I think I learned a lot more than I would have done at film school, for example, because I was getting to make films at the same time. Your film class is the only film class I've done in my entire life.'

you learn as you go. And with a smaller portion of time (if any) dedicated to real-world experiences, it can become harder to absorb and vividly remember what you learn, or to integrate the learning into real life.

All in all then, university can be an excellent route if you enjoy studying conceptual knowledge. However, there's often less exposure to practical learning. This means that you may have to compensate for this weakness with internships or other types of work experience during the holidays, if you wish to stand out from other graduates.

> ### Exercise: Do I have a preference for an academic path?
>
> To find out if you have a preference for conceptual learning or for a practical education, take some time to consider the following questions, and make a note of your answers.
>
> **Note**: As already mentioned, no one is 100% an academic or practical learner. The questions below only help to identify which way you *lean*. Learning preferences can also change across time or subjects. For now, though, focus on how you would like to carry on learning when you leave school.
>
> | | |
> |---|---|
> | Do you mostly enjoy learning in a classroom and in a well-ordered fashion, as opposed to learning in an exploratory hands-on fashion? | Yes/No |
> | Do you tend to think about and work through ideas before putting them into practice, rather than do things first and reflect on them later? | Yes/No |
> | Do you enjoy reading and studying new knowledge for intellectual curiosity, rather than for immediate application? | Yes/No |
> | Do you prefer a measured pace of learning, as opposed to a fast-moving environment? | Yes/No |
> | Do you prefer to be tested on your knowledge through exams and essays, rather than practical workshops and live assessments? | Yes/No |
>
> If you answered 'yes' to most of the questions above, a traditional university degree might be a more suitable path for you than an apprenticeship.

Apprenticeships and the Practical Path

Apprenticeships have a long history of being focussed on practical knowledge in areas such as manufacturing, engineering and construction. Today, apprenticeships have grown beyond these industries, but the learning approach remains practical. The approach is especially powerful because you get to use newly acquired knowledge in real-life situations more or less straight away, rather than having to wait until after graduation. You also get live feedback on the knowledge that you're accumulating. Because of this, many people find that the theory that you learn during an apprenticeship can be easier to remember and internalise.

We've already looked at two examples of how well practical learning works (learning how to speak as a toddler and learning how to be a pilot), but let's consider one more example to further illustrate the point.

When you start driving lessons you might expect to spend roughly 60 hours on the road (or less if you're really good!). In this time, you effectively learn how to drive by driving. In contrast, you'll spend just 10 to 20 hours learning driving *theory*. This is because, to be a good driver, you can't rely on theory alone. You do better by being on the road a lot, seeing new traffic situations and being guided on how to deal with them in real time.

As we saw in Chapter 5, this kind of practical learning is the most dominant aspect of apprenticeships, which are made up of 80% on-the-job learning versus just 20% off-the-job learning (in the form of theory classes and coaching).

Although apprenticeships offer a faster way of learning practical skills, there can be challenges. For example, given that you spend the majority of your time doing real work for an employer, this leaves you with less time to reflect on learnings and to explore the best theoretical knowledge that could be applied. Also, some apprenticeships might not have the same quality of theoretical training that you will generally get through an established degree course (although many apprenticeship programmes these days actually involve attending colleges and universities for off-the-job learning anyway).

Apprentice Perspective

Sophie Adelman, Co-founder of Multiverse

Multiverse is an organisation that trains and matches apprentices to employers. It prepares young people for roles in a wide range of businesses, ranging from Santander and L'Oréal to Mercedes-Benz and Just Eat. When asked about how apprentices learn, here's how Sophie Adelman, one of the founders of the company, explained a key concept to me:

'Apprenticeships will teach you some skills, but then you have to go and apply those skills in the workplace and in a different context. That application of knowledge and skills in a workplace environment, in a real-life setting, means that you have to adapt, and that actually teaches you how to learn.

'If you think about it, what is learning how to learn? Learning how to learn is "How do I apply something theoretical, practically?", "How do I transfer knowledge?", "How do I look for the information I need?"

'Software engineering is a great example – you can learn the syntax of software, you can learn the different elements of how to write algorithms, but actually, most of the time developers have to go on GitHub or Reddit and seek an insight into how to solve a problem. It's not something they can just pull off from a textbook that tells you exactly how to do it.

'So I think apprenticeships are actually very good [for this] – the idea of applied learning. That is the heart of all our apprenticeships.'

That said, if you like being hands-on and learning as you go, an apprenticeship can be both a fun and effective way to develop your knowledge and skills. In addition, if you feel you need to, you can always make time to boost your theoretical knowledge through independent learning after you're qualified.

Exercise: Do I have a preference for practical learning?

To find out if you have a preference for practical, hands-on learning over the conceptual, academic approach, take some time to consider the following questions and make a note of your answers.

Reminder: As already mentioned, no one is 100% either a practical or an academic learner. The questions below only help to identify which way you lean. Learning preferences can also change across time or subjects. For now, though, focus on how you would like to carry on learning when you leave school.

Do you enjoy learning through immediate practical work, rather than reading books or listening to a teacher?	Yes/No
Are you comfortable learning in a fast-paced, real-life work environment, rather than in a classroom or lecture hall?	Yes/No
Are you comfortable getting tasks done under pressure in a fast-paced environment, yet you are still able to set time aside to study?	Yes/No
Do you enjoy taking ownership of your personal development outside of what is expected of you at school and in other areas?	Yes/No
Do you prefer your knowledge to be tested through practical tasks, rather than theoretical tests or exams?	Yes/No

If you answered yes to most of the questions, an apprenticeship could be the better path for you.

Establishing the Right Choice for You – based on Learning Preferences

To learn anything well, you have to both be able to understand it in a *theoretical* way and be able to *apply* the knowledge in the real world. This means that, whatever route you choose to take after school, you will benefit from both the theoretical and the practical learning involved.

However, as university tends to involve more academic learning while apprenticeships favour a more practical approach, it means that a decision between university and an apprenticeship is also a decision between more theory or more practice. And, ultimately, only you can decide which of these two approaches feels right for *you*.

Chapter Recap

▶ Some people prefer to learn academically while others prefer to learn practically. It can be useful to explore your *own* learning preferences to help you decide what route to take after school.

▶ To be an effective learner you have to draw on *both* types of learning, but for the most part, practical learning does a better job of getting you ready for the real world.

▶ University favours academic learning, so a degree is often a better path for people who enjoy studying conceptual knowledge and thinking in a theoretical capacity.

▶ If you're more practically inclined, an apprenticeship is often a better match. This route offers more opportunities to learn how to think about and respond to situations in the real world of work.

10
THE FINANCIAL COSTS

You will probably have seen the headlines about the skyrocketing costs of a university education. 'Students are racking up six-figure debts after taking out huge loans to pay for higher education, official figures show,' went one *Daily Mail* headline; 'Student debt rising to more than £50,000, says IFS,' went another from the BBC.

Average loan balance for graduates who are due to start paying back their loans

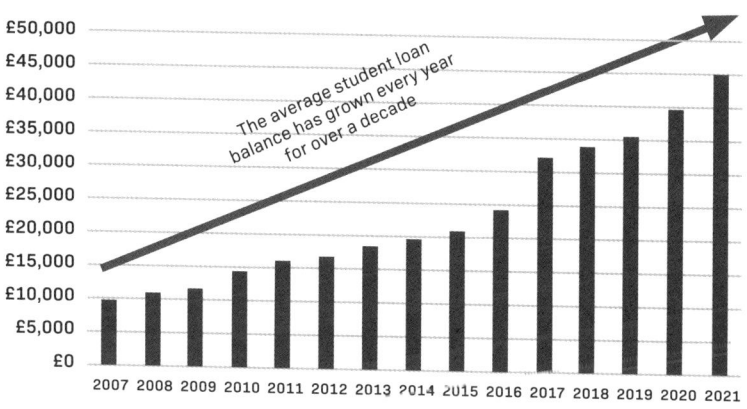

(Data Source: Student Loans Company)

These reports can be shocking, and they rightly highlight the issue of the rising cost of a degree. The graph on page 131 shows how each new set of UK graduates end up with more student debt as the years go on. (Graduates who started repaying their loans in 2007 had an average outstanding balance of just £10,000, while those who started repaying their loans in 2021 – so students who graduated in 2020 – had an average balance of £45,000 to pay off.)

But it's important to take dramatic headlines like the ones just mentioned with a pinch of salt. They can exaggerate the reality in some ways and miss out key facts about how student loans work. After all, they're different to bank loans. The news headlines also represent a one-sided view of things that doesn't take into account the potential *earnings* of graduates – a significant portion of whom are financially better off in the long term (see Chapter 11).

So while the dramatic headlines are somewhat justified by the rapid rise in the costs of a degree, we have to fully understand the nature of student debt before passing further judgement on whether going to university is still worth the price.

With that in mind, we'll spend a lot of this chapter looking at how student loans work, and the impact that they can have on your future earnings, as well as considering both the tuition fees and living costs involved in going to university. Since there are no tuition fees for an apprenticeship we won't spend as much time on that route. We also won't cover the costs of other career paths, because even though other routes could be cheaper, the costs are too varied to cover them all in this chapter.

Note that, although this chapter aims to include information relating to the cost of a degree in all regions of the UK (i.e. England, Scotland, Wales and Northern Ireland), the main focus is England. This is for the sake of clarity in the numerical examples provided. However, you can use the same maths for the figures relating to whichever region you are from in order to work out the overall costs that would apply to *you*.

> **Insight**
>
> **Finding out university costs**
>
> Tuition fees are always subject to change by the government. To get the latest figures, be sure to visit www.gov.uk/student-finance. It's also worth looking at the UCAS guide on the topic at www.ucas.com/money.

The Cost of a University Education

University has two main costs: tuition fees and living expenses, so let's look at each one a little more closely.

Tuition fees

Tuition fees in England have been around £9,000 a year for domestic students since 2012 – that was the year when they tripled from just £3,000 in prior years. Today, most universities charge £9,250 annually. However, it's always worth checking specific course details in case they're different. Some universities also offer accelerated degrees, which run for two years instead of three, and therefore cost less. Otherwise for most students in England, a three-year degree will cost £27,750 in tuition fees alone.

Tuition fees may vary in the other regions of the UK – as shown by the 2021–2022 figures in the table on page 134. So if you're from one of these regions, feel free to substitute the cost relevant to you instead of the English costs used in this chapter.

Region of the UK	2021-2022 Academic Year
	Tuition fees for resident students in the region
England	Up to £9,250 per year
Scotland	No fees for Scottish residents; otherwise, fees can be up to £9,250
Wales	Up to £9,250 per year
Northern Ireland	Up to £4,530 per year

Insight

The opportunity costs of going to university

When you go to university, you incur tuition fees (as outlined above) rather than take the opportunity to earn a salary as part of an apprenticeship or through a full-time job. Economists call this type of 'invisible' cost an 'opportunity cost' – so-called as it represents the potential benefit, or 'opportunity', that you lose by doing something else.

So can we put a cash value on this hidden cost in the context of university versus apprenticeships? Well, it's hard to be exact, but we can hazard a rough guess ...

Taking a talented Higher Apprentice as a point of comparison, this person could earn as much as £20,000 in a full year. But since we want to make the comparison to a university student, let's assume that the period of time we are concerned with is similar to an academic year – roughly nine months – which would bring the apprentice's earnings down to £15,000 for the period in hand.

Once you deduct taxes, the apprentice would end up with around £13,900 of earnings. However, before we can arrive at an 'opportunity cost', we also have to deduct expenses that are common to both university *and* apprenticeship paths. In this case, we can assume the same living expenses for both paths (roughly £8,800), with both the student and apprentice living away from home. After deducting living

CHAPTER 10 THE FINANCIAL COSTS

Living expenses

Now let's look at living expenses, such as accommodation, food, travel, socialising and other bits you need at uni. Everyone has a different lifestyle so total living costs will vary from person to person. However, we can still look at some averages to give you a rough guide as to how much it might cost you.

expenses from the £13,900 of after-tax earnings, you arrive at an opportunity cost of roughly £5,100 for each academic year of university.

So if you choose the university route when you could have realistically also secured a Higher Apprenticeship, you theoretically also forgo £5,100 a year. (This assumes you aren't working while at university.) After graduation from a standard three-year course, the total opportunity cost of university could therefore be £15,300.

Theoretically, this means that university doesn't just cost the headline figure of around £50,000 in England and Wales. It may also cost you roughly another £15,000 or more in the form of opportunity costs, and that's before we consider the interest rates on student loans (more on this later).

This brings the total theoretical cost of university to just over £65,000 (i.e. £50,000 plus £15,000).

Now, if going to university can cost that much, can it possibly be worth it, financially? To answer that question fully we have to take a longer-term view by looking at how the lifetime earnings of a graduate minus the university costs (i.e. the 'net lifetime earnings') might compare to those of a Higher Apprentice, so this is something we'll return to in Chapter 11.

IS GOING TO UNI WORTH IT?

According to a 2021 survey by Save the Student, the average weekly accommodation cost for students in the UK is £146 (or £152 for London). A typical accommodation contract for nine months at university would therefore amount to £5,256 (or £5,472 for London).

Another survey from the same organisation reported that students in the UK spent an average of £389 per month on all other expenses (food, going out, transport, bills, clothes, etc.). So that's at least another £3,501 over the nine months while you're living at university rather than home.

Putting these two costs together (£5,256 for rent and £3,501 for other expenses) means that each year of university may cost at least £8,757. A three-year degree in the UK would then amount to £26,271 in living costs alone.

The total bill

Using the numbers in the previous section, if we add the total tuition fees (of £27,750 in England) to the total living costs (£26,271) of university over three years, the total cost of a degree in England would come to £54,021.

In some cases, the total bill can be lower. For example, if you live in a less expensive part of the country, or if you find particularly good value accommodation, you will save money; and it's much, much cheaper, of course, if you opt to live at home while you study. On the other hand, the bill could be higher if you opt to live in London – a city where living costs exceed national averages. And, no matter where you live, your total bills can rise rapidly if you lead a more extravagant life than most. Roughly speaking though, and for the rest of this chapter, we'll assume that a three-year degree would cost at least £54,000 in England or Wales. Meanwhile, remember that residents of Scotland and Northern Ireland might pay a lot less! (See the tuition fee table on page 134.)

CHAPTER 10 THE FINANCIAL COSTS

How Student Loans Work

In the previous sections we worked out that a three-year degree may cost you £54,000 in England or Wales (or less, depending on where in the UK you are resident and where you choose to go to university). Since this is a huge amount of money that only a few people could independently afford, the UK government offers funding in the form of both tuition fee loans and maintenance loans. These loans work differently to traditional bank debt and have a number of benefits. But first, let's go over the basics.

Tuition fee loans

You can apply for a tuition fee loan through Student Finance England, Student Awards Agency for Scotland, Student Finance Wales or Student Finance Northern Ireland depending on which one is relevant to you. Each of these is a department of the government-run organisation The Student Loans Company (SLC), which administers student loans. Eligible applicants can get **up to £9,250** per academic year and these sums are sent directly to the university (not into your personal bank account).

More information can be found on the following websites, depending on the region you'll be in:
- ▶ **England** Student Finance England: www.gov.uk/student-finance
- ▶ **Scotland** Student Awards Agency for Scotland: www.saas.gov.uk
- ▶ **Wales** Student Finance Wales: www.studentfinancewales.co.uk
- ▶ **Northern Ireland** Student Finance Northern Ireland: www.studentfinanceni.co.uk

Maintenance loans

To help cover your living costs, you can also apply for a maintenance loan. This money is paid directly into your bank account in instalments at the beginning of each term. You can, of course, spend this money as you wish, but it's meant to cover your living expenses such as rent, food and travel.

Over the years, the size of these loans has increased as student living costs have risen. The average maintenance loan for students in the UK who started university in 2015 was £4,000 per year, but a more recent report in 2021 by Save the Student put this figure at around £5,640.

The exact amount that you can get is determined by personal circumstances. These include how much your parents earn, whether you decide to live at home or not, and whether you study in London or outside the capital.

For example, a London-based student from a relatively low-income household who doesn't live at home could get up to £12,300 a year. In contrast, a student who comes from a high-income household and who stays at home for a university course outside of London might get £3,500 per year.

The table opposite summarises the maximum maintenance loans available to students, depending on their long-term place of residence at the time of applying for university. To find the latest figures, check out the student finance calculator at *www.gov.uk/student-finance-calculator*.

Tuition fee + maintenance loans

The total student debt of a graduate from England will be the sum of:

CHAPTER 10 THE FINANCIAL COSTS

- the tuition fee loan (up to £9,250 per year)
- the maintenance loan (up to £12,382 per year)
- interest (more on this later).

So if your tuition fees are £9,250 per year, and you take up the average annual maintenance loan of £5,640 that we identified earlier, your total student debt before interest would be roughly £45,000. For students taking up larger maintenance loans (and many people fall into this camp), the bill before interest can be well over £50,000.

Maximum Maintenance Loan (2021–2022 Academic Year)				
(Check www.gov.uk for the latest annual figures)				
Personal Situation	England	Wales	Scotland (Loans & Bursary)	Northern Ireland
Living at home	£7,987	£8,790	£5,750 & £2,000	£3,750
Living away from home, outside London	£9,488	£10,350	£5,750 & £2,000	£4,840
Living away from home, in London	£12,382	£12,930	£5,750 & £2,000	£6,780
If you spend a year of a UK course abroad	£10,866	£8,810	£5,750 & £2,000	£5,770

Repaying a student loan

Tuition fee and maintenance loans can be treated as one lump sum since they are paid back in the same way. In this section we'll simply refer to this total as the student loan.

As with most loans, student debt has three important features:

1. the **loan term** (the time within which the loan has to be repaid)

2. **interest** (basically the extra bit you give back in addition to what you borrowed)
3. and **repayments** (the regular payments you make to gradually take the loan sum down to zero).

However, student loans are different to traditional bank loans across these features, and this works out to your benefit. Here's why.

The loan term (30 years)

If you aren't in a position to pay back your student loan within 30 years after graduation (see the 'Repayments' section on page 142 for more on this), the government will cancel your debt. Whatever balance is left at the end of that period gets written off and you will owe nothing thereafter. (In contrast, if you don't pay back a bank loan within the loan term, the lender can take you to court.)

One statistic that's worth knowing is that, based on the current student loan system, most graduates are not able to repay their loans in full. Figures from the Institute of Fiscal Studies show that the government expects to recoup its money plus interest from roughly just one in five students.

Interest (3% to 6%)

The basic concept of interest is simple. If you borrow £100 and annual interest is 5%, after one year you'll owe £105. In the second year – assuming you haven't paid anything back yet – another 5% interest is applied to the new balance of £105 so that you then owe £110.25 (see table below.)

Interest Rate Example	First Year	Second Year
Starting Balance	£100.00	£105.00
Interest of 5% Applied	+ £5.00	+ £5.25
Closing Balance	£105.00	£110.25

CHAPTER 10 THE FINANCIAL COSTS

A student loan operates in a similar fashion. Once you receive it, interest starts being applied immediately. However, beware that the interest rate changes every year and when you graduate, it can be lower (or higher) depending on your annual income. We'll leave this complexity out here, and instead look at a basic example of how applying a simple rate can affect your loan balance.

If we assumed that the annual interest rate was 5% (the average from 2012 to 2021 was 5.6%) and your student loan balance was £54,000 at the start of the year, the interest added by the end of that year would be about £2,700. This amount of interest may look expensive, but the student loan repayment mechanism makes things more manageable.

Example of interest added to initial loan balance

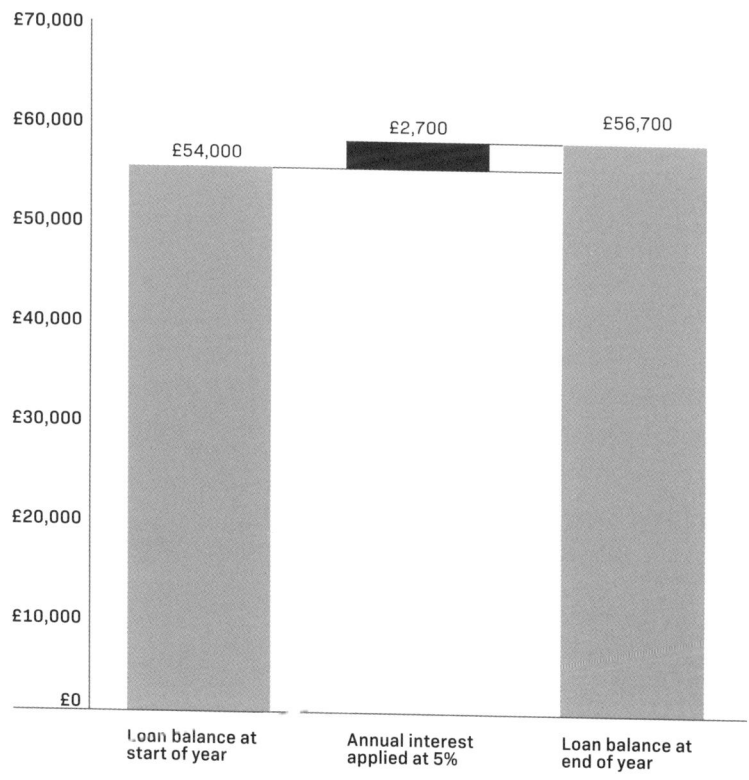

Repayments

A major advantage of student loans is that you don't have to pay *anything* back until you're earning a good salary. Even then, the repayments aren't excessive.

So how are repayments calculated? At the time of writing, graduates from 2020 would only start paying back their student loans if they were earning more than £27,295 a year. The repayment amount that's taken from a graduate's salary is then calculated at a rate of 9% of whatever is earned above the threshold of £27,295. Note: This threshold is for 6 April 2021 to 5 April 2022 and usually rises slightly each year. Be sure to check www.gov.uk/repaying-your-student-loan/what-you-pay for the latest figures.

Repayments are deducted automatically by your employer when you get a job that meets the designated salary level – so there's no way of avoiding them when they're due. In fact, you can think of these repayments like an income tax. (This is how finance guru Martin Lewis explains it on his well-known website, moneysavingexpert.com.) The more you earn, the more you repay.

Let's consider a simple example to see how this works in practice. In the table below, we have used the 2021/22 threshold of £27,295. The student loan repayment is then calculated as 9% of what's earned above that threshold. All numbers are rounded to the nearest pound. Note: If you earned less than £27,295 annually, you wouldn't repay anything.

Graduate Annual Salary	£30,000
Student Loan Repayment Threshold	Must earn more than £27,295 to start repaying
Amount Over the Threshold	£2,705 (i.e. £30,000 minus £27,295)
Repayment Rate	9%
Total Annual Repayment	£243 (i.e. £2,705 x 9%)
Monthly Repayment	£20 (i.e. £243 / 12)

CHAPTER 10 THE FINANCIAL COSTS

The simple table below provides further examples to illustrate how monthly student loan payments change depending on how much you earn.

Annual Salary	Monthly Repayment Estimate
£27,295 or less	No payment
£30,000	£20
£40,000	£95
£50,000	£170
£60,000	£245

Note: The average repayment amount for graduates who started paying back their loans in 2021 was just under £30 per month; they've only just started their careers, so their repayments will be low. Meanwhile, graduates from a decade ago who are subject to repayments are likely to now have more senior jobs and higher salaries, so this group is repaying just over £100 a month on average.

Insight
Other sources of funding

Since a maintenance loan might not be enough to cover all living costs, many students get additional financial support from their parents or other family. One survey in 2020 found that parents gave an average of £130 per month to their child to support with university costs.

It's also possible to apply for scholarships or bursaries. These are usually lump sums of money gifted to individuals who meet specific criteria set by the scholarship sponsor. Example criteria include academic talent, athletic ability, diversity of your background, and sometimes a subject combined with place of residence. Make sure you ask the universities you're interested in whether they have any scholarships or bursaries on offer, and also check with your local authority for location-specific scholarships.

So What Does this All Mean?

Let's take a break from the maths for a moment and look at the bigger picture. If there's anything to take from this chapter so far it's this: a university education is certainly expensive, but the student loan that funds it can make that cost manageable in three important ways.

First, you only start paying back a student loan when you're earning a reasonable salary (typically more than about £27,000 a year). So if your degree doesn't lead to a well-paid career, you aren't expected to start paying back what you owe.

> ### Graduate Perspective
>
> #### Francine Quaicoe, Sociology graduate (now a lecturer)
>
> We already met Francine in Chapter 1. Even though she agrees that university is expensive, she also firmly believes that young people should not rule it out just because of the headline student debt figures. There's more to the story, and here's how she sees things:
>
> > 'I know a lot people stress that the disadvantage of going to university is being in debt and spending a lot of money and so forth. But I also feel like that's not an issue, because we need to encourage people to invest in themselves. When you invest in yourself, you're going to have to spend money.
> >
> > 'So we shouldn't put someone off from going to university because it's costly. And if someone says I'm not going to university because it's too expensive, well, I'd say it's an investment. If a job that you want to do requires you to go to university but you don't want to go because it's too expensive, then I would disagree with that.'

Second, when you start earning a higher level salary, the monthly loan repayments are usually small enough not to impact your lifestyle significantly.

Finally, the government doesn't *expect* the majority of graduates to pay back their student loans in full. So, unlike bank debt, no one will come after you if you aren't able to repay your student loan.

> **Insight**
> **How changes in student loan terms can affect the cost of a degree**
>
> The government can modify student loan terms in a way that either increases or decreases the cost of a degree. Although it's hard to predict what these changes will be in the future, the following examples from UK parliament briefings in 2021 highlight what's possible:
>
> - **Loan term** (increase from 30 to 35 years). If the loan term increased by five years, the average total repayment per graduate would increase by 13% (about £3,800 more). Middle- to higher-earning graduates would be impacted the most, with an increase of total repayments of £7,800.
> - **Repayment rate** (incresae from 9% to 10%). If the repayment rate increased to 10%, the average total repayment per graduate would rise by almost 6% (or £1,600). Again, middle- to higher-earning graduates would be affected the most, with around £3,000 of extra repayments.
> - **Repayment threshold** (decrease from £27,295 to £25,000). If the salary at which you start repaying student loans falls to £25,000, the average borrower's total repayments would increase by 8% (or £2,500.) In this example, middle-earning graduates would be impacted the most, with extra £4,000 (on average) of extra repayments.

The Cost of an Apprenticeship

The apprenticeship path is simpler when it comes to costs: there are no tuition fees, and you most likely won't need to take on any debt since you will get paid a salary to train with an organisation. However, you'll still have living expenses (and you'll also have to pay tax on your earnings). So if your living costs happen to go beyond your income, you might have to seek some kind of additional support, just as some university students do – whether in the form of financial help from your parents or other family members (if they are in a position to give it) or in the form of a loan or grant of some kind (if you are able to secure one).

However, if you secure a Higher Apprenticeship, for example, and are fortunate enough to earn £20,000 a year, you can expect an income of around £17,300 after taxes, based on UK tax rates at the time of writing. If you're living away from home and have roughly similar living costs to a university student, you can deduct roughly another £12,300 for accommodation and other personal expenses for a full calendar year (versus the £8,800 estimated earlier for the nine months of a university year). This would leave you with roughly £5,000 a year to save or spend – not bad at all for continuing your learning after school.

The Right Choice for You – based on Financial Costs

If we look at just the headlines, university appears way more expensive compared to the apprenticeship route. You're likely to graduate with significant student loans to pay back after a degree, and you also forgo the potential to earn income as an apprentice or in the workplace.

CHAPTER 10 THE FINANCIAL COSTS

However, the tuition fees and living costs alone don't tell the full story given that student loans are so manageable — what with you only having to start paying them back once you're earning a salary over a certain level (a little over £27,000 a year at the time of writing); with monthly repayments being small enough not to impact your lifestyle significantly; and with the UK government being willing to write off any remaining student debt after 30 years. This may change in the future but at least for now, student debt isn't as bad as it first appears.

It's also important to look at what a university degree buys you in terms of financial rewards down the line because, as it turns out, many graduates do end up getting a positive financial return from their education. So this aspect of university as an 'investment' in yourself (something that takes a bit of foresight to put figures on) will be the focus of the next chapter.

In conclusion, however, if it came down to making a choice between university and apprenticeships on the basis of costs alone, the main question to answer would be this: would you rather start earning now (assuming you can secure a good apprenticeship) or would you be comfortable with a student loan that can help you get a degree with good earning potential, but which leads to monthly salary deductions of around £20–£100 for many years?

Chapter Recap

▶ University has two main costs: tuition fees (up to £9,250 per year) and living expenses (around £8,800 per year).

▶ Student loans are widely available that will cover your tuition fees as well as most of your living costs. This makes university accessible to many people.

▶ If you choose to go to university and need a student loan to cover the costs, you'll need to accept that you'll have monthly deductions from your salary to repay the loan once your income reaches a certain level.

▶ Based on thresholds at the time of writing, monthly repayments don't have to begin until your income is a little over £27,000 a year. However, beware that this threshold is subject to change so always check on this before making a decision.

▶ Any student debt that's still remaining after 30 years gets written off by the government.

▶ Apprenticeships are generally a better option in terms of cost alone, given that you get paid for being trained, rather than paying for it.

11
THE FUTURE FINANCIAL REWARDS

Since tuition fees tripled from £3,000 to £9,000 in 2012, the proportion of students who believe they get good value for money from their time at university has been on a downward trend (see the solid grey line in the chart below).

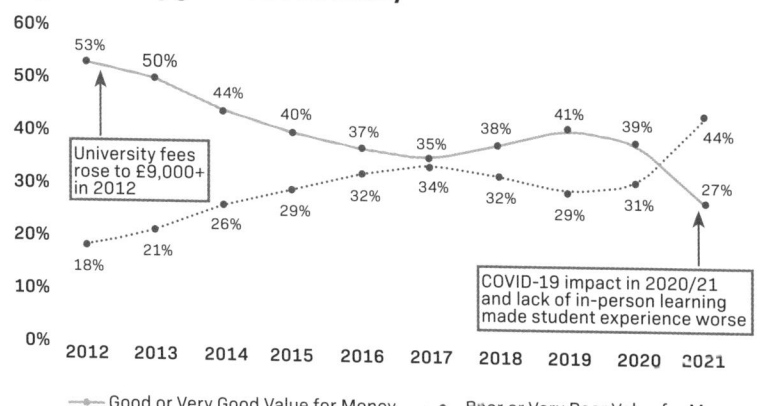

Percentage of students who report university is good or very good value for money

> ## Insight
> ### It's not all about the numbers
>
> It's important to remember that your decision about what to do after school shouldn't be based on numbers alone. This chapter may contain lots of figures, but that doesn't make these the most important thing; they're only one factor. Here's why:
>
> - **Education isn't just about money**. You've been able to read this book because of your education. You can appreciate art and music more when you learn what goes into it. You can work with people better when you understand human psychology. Being well-educated (whether that's through university, an apprenticeship or another path) isn't just about enabling you to build financial wealth – it can make life richer in many *other* ways too.
> - **Long-term statistics are estimates**. There are many assumptions that go into producing statistics, and just by changing a few key assumptions you can end up with wildly different outcomes. For example, if the government decided to scrap interest rates on student loans, the overall cost of a degree would fall quite considerably. So, when thinking about this chapter remember that numbers are just estimates that provide one of many parts to a story.
> - **The world is always changing**. By the time you read this book many things may have changed. For example, the COVID-19 pandemic had an enormous impact on the economy, and that had a markedly negative impact on graduates and apprentices. However, new training and learning options that provide *better* value may emerge in the future. For instance, the Degree Apprenticeship mentioned earlier in the book, which makes it possible to get the best of the rewards of both an apprenticeship and a university education combined – wasn't an option until 2015.

As you can see from the chart, it's now been a long time that a high percentage of students have felt that they do not receive good or very good value for money from university. This was made even worse in 2021 at the height of the COVID-19 pandemic when

CHAPTER 11 THE FUTURE FINANCIAL REWARDS

in-person learning and social life on university campuses became so restricted. In that year, just 27% of UK students believed they were getting their money's worth, while 44% thought university was poor or very poor value for money.

However, findings like this, which are only ever from one given point in time, shouldn't be considered in isolation, as the financial rewards of a degree often come later – in a cumulative way.

In this chapter we will therefore look at the long-term financial rewards of university and how they compare to those of apprenticeships. As in the previous chapter assessing costs, we will not be going into detail about alternative paths here, such as going straight from school into work, as they aren't as easy to compare and we just don't have the space. However, if this is a path you are considering, my hope is that you can glean enough from the analytical processes used here in order to do some research and comparative work of your own.

Before we crack on, a key message that you'll find in this chapter, and one that you'll want to remember, is this: over the long term, both graduates and those who complete higher-level apprenticeships have the potential for healthy financial rewards. In fact, as you'll see on page 164, where a chart shows lifetime earnings of people who have taken different paths after school, the differences aren't as large as you might expect. Moreover, there are some situations where former apprentices earn more than graduates, and vice versa.

Ultimately, how well you go on to do in your career will depend on a whole range of factors, some of which will be within your control, such as how much effort you put into your learning, development and career progress, while others may be outside of your control – such as who you happen to meet when, what opportunities you come across and the like.

The key to 'success' on whatever path you take will be to approach it with a positive mindset, sincere effort and attention. By giving it your best and keeping an eye out for good opportunities, you will reap the rewards that you deserve.

What Do Graduates Earn?

Many people go to university with the hope that they'll get a well-paid job at the end of their course. In Chapter 4 we saw that the prospects of getting a job after university are indeed good. (We also saw in Chapter 5 that a higher proportion of apprentices than students are in work after their qualification.)

But when it comes to financial rewards in the long run, does university pay off compared to if you went straight into work after your A levels without further qualifications? On average, the answer is yes.

According to research commissioned by the UK Department for Business, Innovation and Skills, the average graduate earns around £100,000 extra over a working life compared to someone who only has A levels. This is the 'net benefit', so it's the total benefit after removing taxes and the costs of a degree.

In another report published by the Institute for Fiscal Studies (IFS) in 2020, the lifetime earnings of university graduates were estimated to be 20% higher than those who had just GCSE and A level qualifcations. This translated to *extra* net lifetime earnings in the range of £100,000 to £130,000. (Unfortunately, this report, as with so many others like it, does not consider apprenticeships.)

There are more statistics along these lines that, although varied, all generally point in the same direction: that of a degree usually paying off financially in the end.

It's important to emphasise that the £100,000 benefit is an average. This so-called 'graduate premium' – in other words the financial benefit of a degree – can be vastly different depending on a range of factors. Some of these factors are beyond your influence, such as the health of the economy and how many graduate job vacancies are available. But other factors can be within your sphere of influence: what you decide to study, where you decide to study, and what grade you achieve on graduation. Let's examine each of these further.

The course you choose

Before we get to the numbers, let's briefly consider an important definition: Each year the UK's Department of Education ('DoE') shares data on the 'median' earnings of graduates. This number, which is taken from the middle of the full range of graduate earnings, and therefore tells us that half of graduates earn more than this number while the other half earn less, gives a fuller picture than what the arithmetic mean of earnings would. Here's how the numbers stack up.

Figures published in 2021 by the DoE showed that the median annual earnings for graduates were £20,800 one year after university and £27,400 after five years. This means that one year after graduation, half of graduates earned less than £20,800 a year and the other half earned more than this amount. And five years after graduation, half of students were earning less than £27,400 a year and the other half were earning more than that.

However, there are often differences in earnings based on the subject that you choose to study. For example, one year after university, the median annual earnings for Medicine and Dentistry graduates is £36,500, whereas the median for Performing Arts graduates is £14,300. Four years later, these numbers rise to

£49,300 for Medicine and Dentistry (see the top entry in the chart below) and £21,200 for Performing Arts students (see the bottom entry in the chart below).

Graduate median earnings after five years (by subject)

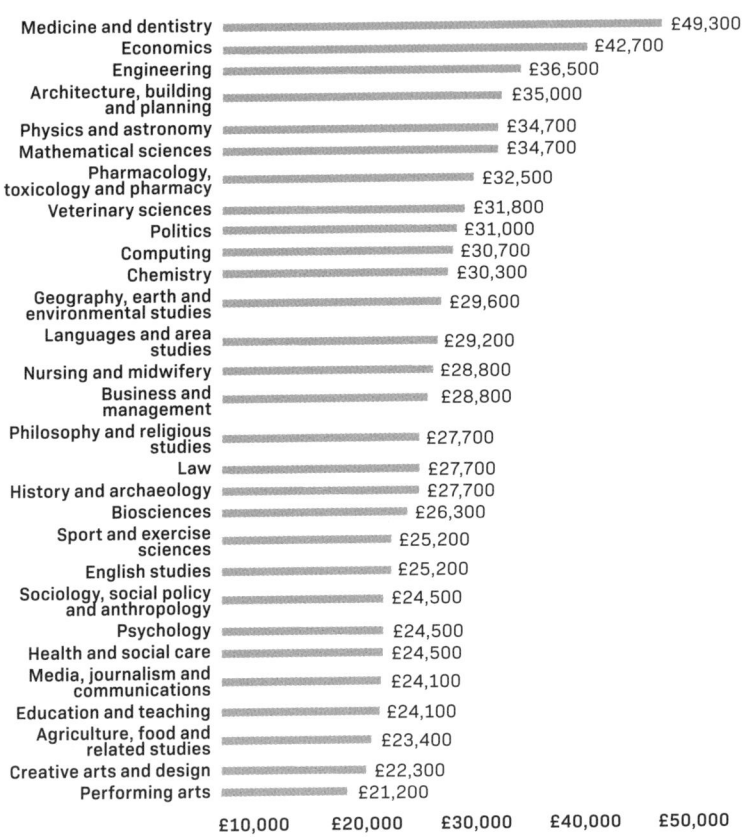

Subject	Earnings
Medicine and dentistry	£49,300
Economics	£42,700
Engineering	£36,500
Architecture, building and planning	£35,000
Physics and astronomy	£34,700
Mathematical sciences	£34,700
Pharmacology, toxicology and pharmacy	£32,500
Veterinary sciences	£31,800
Politics	£31,000
Computing	£30,700
Chemistry	£30,300
Geography, earth and environmental studies	£29,600
Languages and area studies	£29,200
Nursing and midwifery	£28,800
Business and management	£28,800
Philosophy and religious studies	£27,700
Law	£27,700
History and archaeology	£27,700
Biosciences	£26,300
Sport and exercise sciences	£25,200
English studies	£25,200
Sociology, social policy and anthropology	£24,500
Psychology	£24,500
Health and social care	£24,500
Media, journalism and communications	£24,100
Education and teaching	£24,100
Agriculture, food and related studies	£23,400
Creative arts and design	£22,300
Performing arts	£21,200

Such stark differences in financial rewards in relation to subject choices can't be looked at in isolation though. After all, not everyone wants to become a doctor or dentist, plus many people who choose these kinds of high-paying professions don't necessarily do it just for the money. Furthermore, although arts graduates may have lower median earnings, it doesn't mean they

CHAPTER 11   THE FUTURE FINANCIAL REWARDS

can't be as satisfied with or as successful in their careers in other non-financial ways.

Returning to the numbers though, the key thing to remember is that merely having a degree doesn't mean you'll automatically do well financially. As you might remember from earlier chapters, the IFS estimates that one in five UK students would be better off financially by *not* going to university at all. So be mindful about expectations on financial rewards. Some courses lead to higher earnings because of the high-paying careers they are connected to, such as medicine, finance, sciences and technology; others lead to more modest financial outcomes; and others may not lead to easily predicted financial rewards, given that around two thirds of all graduates go on to choose jobs that are unrelated to their degree subject (although this is not to say that they don't do well in a whole host of ways, of course).

The university you get into

It's no surprise that graduates from what are considered the top universities generally do better financially (see the Russell Group list on page 156 for a list of 24 leading universities in the UK). A report from the IFS in 2017 found that five years after graduation, the median annual earnings of graduates from the University of Oxford, Cambridge University and the London School of Economics were over £40,000. In contrast, the lowest-ranked universities in the IFS report had graduates with annual earnings well below £20,000.

Does this mean going to a top university pays off more? In some ways, yes. Having a big-name university brand on your CV can open many doors. But there's a nuance here that's important to think about: a good chunk of the differences in earning potential comes down to the original ability of a student. The top universities have

> **Insight**
>
> **What are Russell Group universities?**
>
> The Russell Group comprises 24 leading universities in the UK that banded together in 1994 to promote world-class research and teaching. The institutions in the Russell Group are known for their higher-than-average teaching quality and graduate job prospects. They are some of the most competitive universities to get into.
>
> - University of Birmingham
> - University of Bristol
> - University of Cambridge
> - Cardiff University
> - Durham University
> - University of Edinburgh
> - University of Exeter
> - University of Glasgow
> - Imperial College London
> - King's College London
> - University of Leeds
> - University of Liverpool
> - London School of Economics
> - University of Manchester
> - Newcastle University
> - University of Nottingham
> - University of Oxford
> - Queen Mary University of London
> - Queen's University Belfast
> - University of Sheffield
> - University of Southampton
> - University College London
> - University of Warwick
> - University of York

competitive processes that aim to identify people who already have a lot of potential, and who have a strong commitment to working hard to get the best out of their learning environments.

This means that while a prestigious university can make your CV stand out, a big part of your success will come from other factors too, including your existing potential and how you demonstrate it.

Certainly, if you can evidence your potential to the world by making it through a competitive process to get into a prestigious university, that's great. But if you don't have access to that path, you can still do well financially without a big-brand university. For instance, over 70% of the UK's richest people who went to university didn't attend any of the leading institutions in the country (see the box on page 156 for a list of these).

The grade you get

Competition for graduate jobs has become fierce as more and more students go to university. So much so that graduates today have to find more ways to stand out to get the best opportunities on offer.

One way to stand out is to graduate with at least an upper second-class degree (known as 'a 2.1'), although a first-class degree (known as 'a First') would be even more beneficial. Researchers have found that there's an employment advantage to higher marks at university. For example, one group of economists found that getting a First instead of a 2.1 increased the average chances of working in a high-wage industry by 13%.

But this, too, has nuances. It turns out that getting a top grade in a more mathematical subject, such as Statistics or Physical Sciences, is linked to different outcomes compared to getting a top grade in an essay-based degree, such as Philosophy. Although a higher grade is always better no matter what you study, economists found that getting a First in a more mathematical subject boosted the chances of high-wage employment by 22%, whereas getting a First in a *non*-maths-based subject only boosted them by 10%.

One possible reason for this is that employers in high-paying and competitive fields apply the crude method of giving more credit to strong grades from maths-based subjects and slightly less credit to strong marks in non-maths subjects.

IS GOING TO UNI WORTH IT?

Another trend that motivates employers to look for even higher marks today is that the proportion of students getting the higher-grade degrees has been on the up, as can be seen in the chart below. For example, while around 60% of graduates got a First or a 2.1 in 2008, that number rose to 82% in 2020. As more people graduate with a First or a 2.1 (which is four in five graduates today), it's more important than ever that if you go to university, you do your best not to fall outside of this category and graduate with a lower grade, i.e. either a lower second-class degree (2.2) or a third-class degree (a Third). Most graduate jobs ask for a 2.1 or higher, so without it, you'd have to demonstrate your abilities in other exceptional ways to stand out. This might include things like strong work experience and other non-academic achievements.

What class of degree have students achieved in the past?
Percentage of graduates getting each degree classification

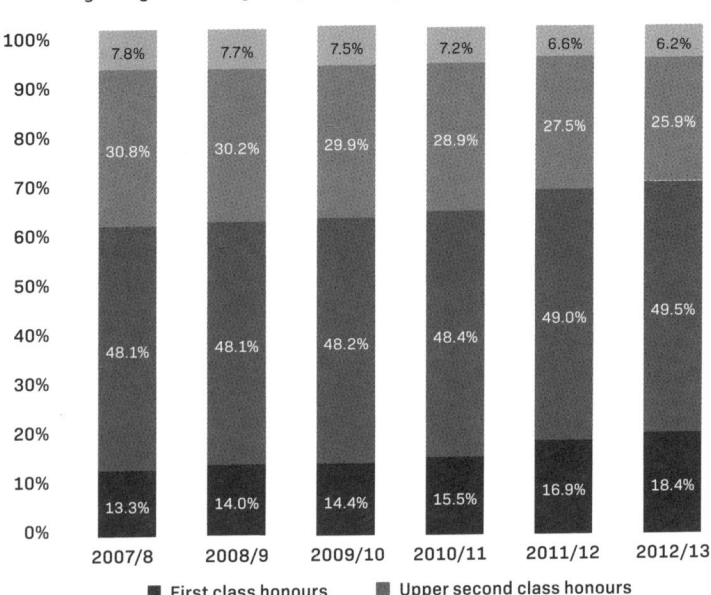

CHAPTER 11   THE FUTURE FINANCIAL REWARDS

So, does a university degree pay off?

Even though there's a lot to consider here, the broad message can be boiled down to one sentence and probably something that you already knew intuitively: graduating with a degree in a well-established subject, from a well-respected university and with a high grade can pay off handsomely.

It's important, however, to remember that a meaningful portion of financial rewards in any job comes from an underlying quality that we all have access to – the ability to work smart and hard at something that we have a passion for. If you're determined and motivated to succeed, know that you can do just as well financially whatever path you choose to take.

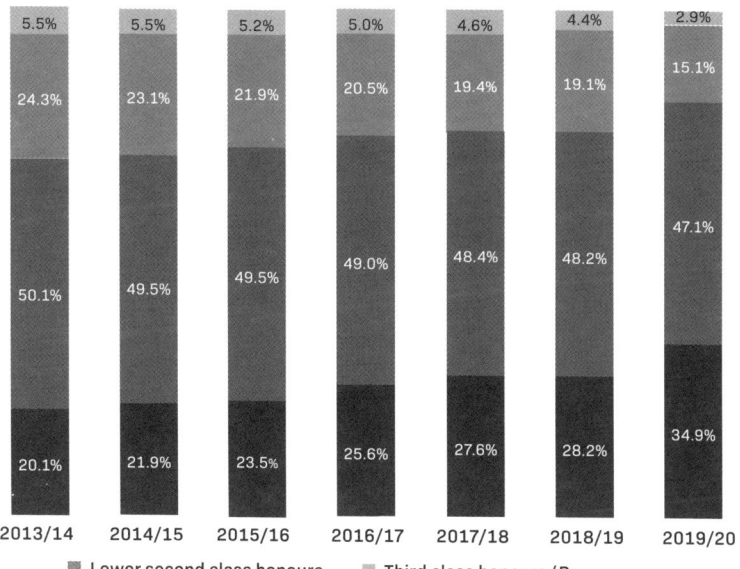

(Data Source: HESA)

> ## Graduate Perspective
>
> ### Darren Tenkorang, Business and Economics graduate (now an entrepreneur)
>
> The rewards of university can go beyond a graduate salary. University of Sussex graduate Darren Tenkorang was always entrepreneurial, but university proved to be a pivotal launch pad for his ambition. On campus, he entered and won a business competition that was sponsored by Santander, and was awarded £10,000 to invest in his app, bringing his business idea to life. Reflecting on what he got out of university, he highlighted one benefit that graduate salary surveys don't capture:
>
> > 'Where I got a lot of value is that, from an entrepreneurial point of view, university is a breeding ground for talent. It's the one place where you can find an accountant, a lawyer, a [software] developer, a marketer, a designer, all in one place... So if you look at it from that perspective, like my management team for example, every single one of them – Head of Operations, Head of Product, and our main [software] developer – they were all at Sussex [with me]. And because I was able to recruit them from when they were at university in their early years, ... I think I got a lot of bang for my buck.'

What do Former Apprentices Earn?

So far we have seen that what you study, where you study it and how well you do in it can impact your earning potential. However, we also know that part of your earning potential is driven by hard work (and some luck too!). But what do the financial returns look like for an apprenticeship compared to a degree?

There maybe isn't as much of a difference as you'd think. Broadly speaking, the earnings you can make in your lifetime as a well-qualified apprentice are not substantially different to those of a graduate.

CHAPTER 11   THE FUTURE FINANCIAL REWARDS

Although detailed estimates of the earnings of those who have completed apprenticeships are hard to come by, research highlights two key factors that are linked to these earnings: (1) the level of apprenticeship qualification and (2) the type of job and industry you work in.

There are other factors that impact pay, such as the organisation that you work for (larger companies usually pay more) and the region that you're based in (Londoners tend to get paid a bit more, although this is generally because the capital is also expensive to live in!). But for now, we'll focus on the levels of apprenticeship and the type of industry.

The levels of apprenticeship

In Chapter 5 we went through the various levels of apprenticeships (see page 65), and I recommended that if you're on track to get your A levels, it's best to aim for the highest level apprenticeships (for example, the Higher and Degree apprenticeship levels). These levels are usually the ones that lead to financial rewards that are comparable to those from a university degree.

We can now put some numbers behind this advice. In 2016, research from Barclays Bank and the Centre for Economics and Business Research (CEBR) estimated that a Level 4 apprentice earns, on average, an extra £117,600 over their working life compared to someone that's only qualified up to A level or equivalent.

This same research found that the figure for graduates was £119,800. According to the Barclays estimates, the difference in earning potential between highly qualified former apprentices and graduates is therefore pretty small, with degree holders earning just 2% more than apprentices on average. (A more recent estimate by the news website MailOnline in 2021 suggested that, after three years of study, apprentices are £52,732 better off than graduates. However, their analysis was more basic and, for example, only considered a three-year earnings period rather than a longer career horizon where total earnings vary more.)

The type of industry

As we've seen at various points throughout the book, a statistical average (or arithmetic mean) across a whole group can mask important nuances, which means it's often helpful to dig deeper to understand what's really going on. This is something that the researchers from the Barclays and CEBR study did by providing data on the lifetime earnings of apprentices and graduates across a *range* of subject areas.

This data revealed that Level 4 apprentices in arts, media and publishing can go on to out-earn those who study an equivalent degree at university by a whopping 270%! At the other end of the spectrum, engineering and business degree holders did better than apprentices by 42%. The chart below highlights such

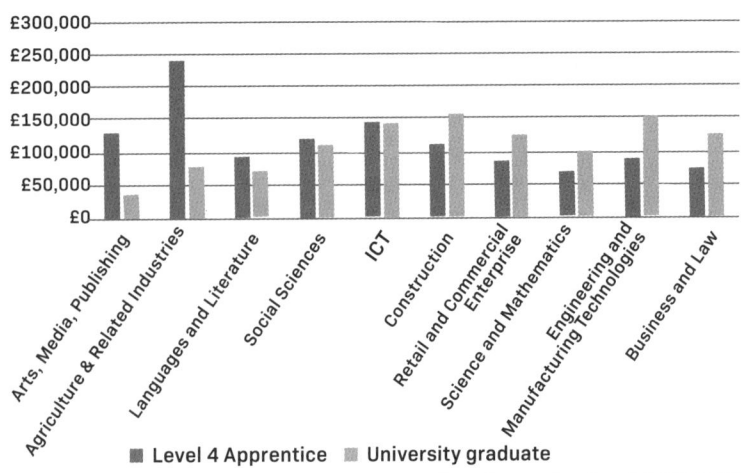

(Data Source: Barclays & CEBR 2016)

differences (the 'earnings premium' is basically the extra portion that people with a degree or apprenticeship earn over people without either qualification).

One factor that drives the difference between arts apprentices and graduates is that, given that this is not a high-salary industry, when you then combine low earnings with student debt, the net lifetime benefit shrinks.

It's also worth noting the impact of work experience. In other words, people who secure an apprenticeship in the arts industry get practical and valuable work experience, build their professional networks and start earning right away, rather than study for three years before getting practical skills and pay. This puts them ahead of lower-earning arts graduates who may struggle to find work in what are often over-subscribed and under-resourced industries.

The experience seems different for business and engineering graduates. The Barclays and CEBR data showed that they generally do better than apprentice equivalents, but this might not be a long-term advantage. It could be that, for now, some employers in the business world prefer recruits from a more *traditional* degree background. However, this is beginning to change as more and more employers recruit candidates from a variety of educational backgrounds.

Apprenticeships versus Universities

We touched on the idea of how graduates from elite universities are linked to higher earnings. Does something similar happen with apprentices? Insightful research on this topic is hard to come by. However, it wouldn't be unrealistic to expect an apprentice at Google in London, for example, to do better financially than an

IS GOING TO UNI WORTH IT?

apprentice at a smaller business outside of the capital. But how about an apprentice compared to a graduate from a highly ranked university?

Research from the Sutton Trust charity in 2015 provides some insights on this question. The organisation compared the estimated total lifetime earnings of people with different types of qualifications across various institutions, and the chart below summarises their findings. (This data assumes you work until age 60 and that degree holders will make their student loan repayments.)

As you can see, this chart shows the average lifetime earnings of people who completed apprenticeships at various levels and of people with degrees from Oxford, Cambridge, Russell Group and non-Russell Group universities.

Surprisingly, the results show that even though Oxford, Cambridge and Russell Group university graduates on average earn more

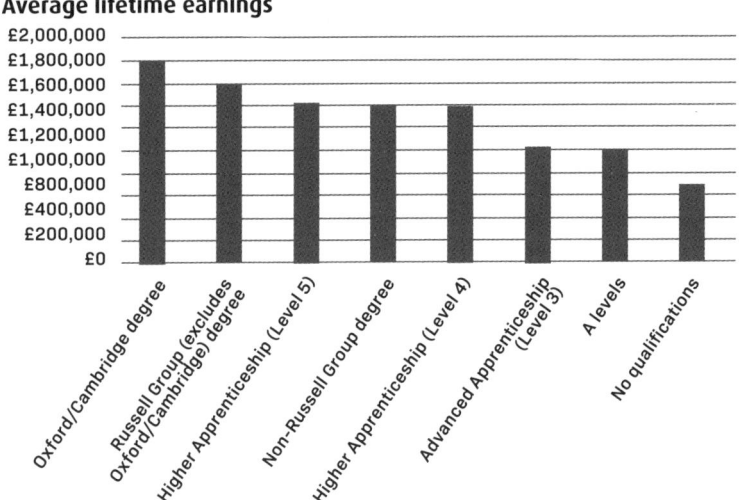

(Data Source: Sutton Trust Report 2015)

than everyone else, the Higher apprentices (Level 5) achieved slightly more lifetime earnings (4% more) than graduates from all other universities. This further dispels the myth that those who complete apprenticeships earn less than graduates.

Also notice in the chart that the lowest lifetime earnings on average were found among people who did not pursue any qualifications equal to or higher than an A level or equivalent. This doesn't mean that if you go straight into work without an apprenticeship you'll do badly; it just means that people who don't go on to train or develop professionally in other ways lose out on average.

In a nutshell, this data shows that over a working life the differences between well-qualified apprentices and graduates aren't as large as people might think. In fact, some apprentices go on to do better than graduates.

The Right Choice for You – based on Future Financial Rewards

It's important to remember that financial rewards are not the be-all-and-end-all when it comes to deciding what to do after school. There are many other aspects of a career that can be fulfilling. These include the type of work you do, the people you work with, where you work and your personal development plans.

That said, we all need financial security so that we can look after ourselves and our loved ones. So it's useful to look at the potential financial rewards of each possible path after school, even if the figures are only a rough estimate that will ebb and flow over the years.

What did the figures in this chapter reveal then? We saw that graduates get an extra £100,000-plus in a lifetime compared to people who only have A levels or equivalent. However, those who qualify at the highest level of apprenticeships can do just as well. In fact, there are cases where former apprentices can end up financially better off than graduates.

In relation to the decision that you're in the throes of making, this means that as long as you aim to do well in *whatever* education or training path you choose to pursue after school, you're likely to be reasonably rewarded for it. However, if you'd like to *maximise* your chances of a high-wage career, university may be the better option if it floats your boat on all other areas, too, of course. You'd just have to aim for a well-respected university, a well-established degree and a 2.1 or higher.

CHAPTER 11 THE FUTURE FINANCIAL REWARDS

Chapter Recap

▶ University graduates earn on average around £100,000 more over a lifetime compared to someone who has only A levels. However, those who qualify at the highest levels of apprenticeships can do just as well financially.

▶ Earnings vary depending on the nature of your education and training. Graduates in some subjects tend to earn more than those in other areas of study, and some apprentices in areas such as the arts go on to do substantially better than graduates of a similar subject.

▶ If a high-wage career is a priority and university appeals to you on all other levels too, an established degree subject at a respected university could be a good option for you. You just have to make sure that you're committed to working hard towards a good grade, which will help you access well-paid job opportunities.

12
YOUR SOCIAL LIFE

If you choose to go to university, you'll be introduced to all sorts of aspects of student life from the get-go during what's called 'freshers' week'. This is a kind of student orientation week at the start of the university year, during which a wide variety of events are held to welcome and orient students. Right from the start of leaving home and family, you'll therefore be thrown into meeting new people, getting to know your campus and accommodation, and plentiful nights out in an exciting new city if you decide to leave your home town.

Beyond freshers' week, you'll be spoilt for choice with all sorts of sports, societies, clubs and events to choose from – which can make the uni experience all the more fun and enriching (albeit that balancing studies and social life can be tricky at times).

Yet, as exciting as freshers' week and university social life are for many, they are not for everyone. A Unite Students survey in 2019 found that UK students, on average, gave freshers' week a 6.5 out of 10 in terms of experience. In fact, just roughly a third of students really enjoyed it. The same survey also revealed that only around a quarter of students believed an active social life to be the most important aspect of a successful student experience.

> ## Graduate Perspective
>
> ## Henry Purchase, Civil Engineering graduate
>
> The COVID-19 pandemic of 2020 changed the nature of social life at university. Freshers' events for that year were cancelled or held in limited form; students had to isolate; and learning shifted online. These measures meant that the vibrant social experience of previous students couldn't be enjoyed by the latest batch of undergraduates, which was a real challenge for many students.
>
> Henry Purchase, a final year Civil Engineering student at the University of Bath, recalls the year and how he used exercise to carry him through:
>
>> 'Covid hit in the first couple of weeks of the second semester after which I immediately moved home and continued my studies online. I was used to online learning, as a combination of my dyslexia and sporting commitments had already made it the best option, so this wasn't a problem for me.
>>
>> 'What did become a problem was losing the social aspect [of university life] as not only did this remove many of the reasons I went to university in the first place, but it also impacted my mental health. To overcome this I (like many others) turned to Zoom to replace social interaction, and I also began running longer distances, which helped me get back the thinking time and mental stimulation that I missed from being in my university city.'

Nevertheless, by giving you direct access to so many varied opportunities, university can certainly spice up your social life, broadening your horizons and giving you a kind of independence that you may have never had until now. Many people make lifelong friends at university, both through their social lives and through their subject courses. But how important is this social aspect in the grand scheme of things? And how might the social life of apprentices compare?

CHAPTER 12 YOUR SOCIAL LIFE

As we've seen in previous chapters, there's no straightforward answers to questions like this but that doesn't mean we can't come to some reasonable conclusions. So in this chapter, we'll briefly look at what your social life might look like at uni versus during an apprenticeship, and we'll consider how this might ultimately affect your decision about what to do next.

Social Life at University

Going to university offers a broad social experience. Many aspects of it are a bit like school in that you get to spend a lot of time with your peers and have plenty of chances to make friends and bond through shared experiences. But you'll get to meet a lot *more* people at uni and many of them will come from more diverse backgrounds. In this sense, university offers a much wider social palette from which you can form new friendships. If you're a person who makes friends easily, you're likely to love this. But, equally, if you struggled to find people who you had something in common with at school, you'll find things easier at university. And here's why…

▶ **Course mates.** A degree intake can have anywhere from a few dozen students to over a hundred. This is often where many lifelong friendships are made since your course mates share the same academic interests as you.

▶ **Flatmates.** Most students live near the university campus in student accommodation or private rental properties. Here you get the opportunity to meet a lot of students from other degree courses who'll be your neighbours during term time.

▶ **Society members.** No one becomes best buddies with everyone on their course or in their student halls. This is where university societies, sports teams and student unions come in. Whatever your hobbies and interests are, there should be a society of students who share these interests and with whom you can socialise. (And if there's no society that covers your interests, you can always start one!)

However, just because university offers a comfortable habitat for social butterflies, it doesn't mean the experience of making new friends is plain sailing for everyone. It takes some effort to speak to new people, but it really is worth it if you want to make the best of what university has to offer.

If you choose to leave home to go to university in a new city, this may also present its own set of challenges in terms of your social life. Some people find it hard to be away from their school friends and others find it hard to stay in touch with them now that their lives have got so busy in other ways. Yet, as many graduates will tell you, some of the friends you've made up to now will still outlast some of those you make at university, so it's good to make the effort to stay in touch as much as you can, without it stopping you from enjoying all the new opportunities on offer.

All said, even though university gives you opportunities to fire up your social life (provided that's something you'd like), you do have to actively engage with this side of things to get the most out of it, and it's important not to forget the people you care about back home as well.

Social Life during Apprenticeships

An apprenticeship doesn't offer the same kind of direct and varied access to social opportunities as university. There's no freshers' week, no on-campus societies to join and no Student

Union bar. And all of this means that the apprenticeship path could risk feeling a bit more like a solo effort, especially if a lot of your school friends head off to university in other cities while you stay at home or move elsewhere for work.

Still, taking the apprenticeship path by no means has to be a lonesome affair. You can still have an active social life across all the following areas:

▶ **Work colleagues.** Although certain professional boundaries need to be respected in work relationships, your colleagues can be a fantastic source of camaraderie and support, especially when it comes to work matters. After all, they'll understand the nature of your job – something you might not necessarily get from your friends outside of work.

▶ **Fellow apprentices.** You may well have fellow apprentices at the firm that employs you (the bigger the organisation, the more chance there will be of this). And if there aren't other apprentices at your workplace, you can still meet some during your training if it's held externally – for example at a college or university.

▶ **Home friends and family.** If you choose an apprenticeship near home, it is easier to stay connected to your family and other friends who have also chosen to stay nearby. And while living at or near home during your apprenticeship (or during university, for that matter) tends to mean less exposure to new people, it allows you to keep up with your existing relationships, minimising the chances of you feeling lonely.

All told, while apprenticeships clearly don't provide the breadth of social opportunities and interactions that university does, there's still the chance to have as much (or little) of a social life as you want.

Apprentice Perspective

Grace Morris, Higher Level Apprentice in Retail Management (now a Deputy Store Manager at Marks and Spencer)

We first learnt about Grace in Chapter 2. She was the first in three generations of her family *not* to go to university. And her bold decision paid off as, having completed a Higher Apprenticeship, she has gone on to quickly rise up the ranks at Marks and Spencer.

As a result, Grace is a huge advocate for apprenticeships. However, she's well aware of some of their weaknesses too:

'The most impactful thing you miss out on with an apprenticeship is having the ease of finding great accommodation. At university, you know everyone around you, you're in the same boat, everyone's new, nervous and young, and you're in a comfort zone. At the age of 17, after finding out I had been chosen for the Marks and Spencer Retail Management programme, I had to go online and find somewhere suitable to live three hours away from my family home in Lincolnshire.

'I chose a modern concept building aimed at young professionals, focussing on "Co-Living", designed much like university halls but with fancier interiors and a gym, library, restaurant and working rooms all located within the building. Of course, this was at an extortionate rent but it gave me a great foundation.

'By going to university you are surrounding yourself with people of the same age with similar interests, most of whom you will form a great connection with and stay friends with for some time. This leads smoothly on to finding a shared house with said mates and, going forward, to easy accommodation with people you know, trust and like.

'This is the biggest difficulty I found with the apprenticeship option – you lack stability in a group of people to live with who are your age if you've moved to a new city or all your friends went to university. I mention this as a big deal because, essentially, it is your social foundation to grow from. And setting yourself up with a good foundation is crucial.'

CHAPTER 12   YOUR SOCIAL LIFE

The Right Choice for You – based on Social Life

University has a lot to offer from a social perspective. It provides you with ready-made opportunities to meet all kinds of new people and take part in all kinds of new activities; many graduates relish the first-year memories of how they met some of their lifelong friends. But not everyone enjoys the social aspect of campus, and it does take effort to rebuild a trusted social circle when you leave home.

The apprenticeship path doesn't offer the same range of social experiences. You can certainly make friends with work colleagues and fellow apprentices, but you're unlikely to have the same diversity of peers as you would at uni. You'll also have to be more proactive in searching out different clubs and the like if you want to pursue particular hobbies or interests outside of work and study.

But how important is this social factor when deciding what path to take after school? Like everything, it really depends on what *you* like and enjoy, what *you'd* like your social life to look like and what you feel would help *you* to thrive. There's no right or wrong here, as everyone is different.

If, when you reflect on this, you realise that you're dying to get out and about as much as possible, meet lots of new, varied people, try lots of new things, and supercharge your social connections in a new setting, then university might be a good fit for you compared to the apprenticeship path. Whereas if the social scene is less important to you, either option could work out well.

However, to be honest, with a little effort, you can carve out whatever kind of social life you would like no matter what path you choose to take after school, so it's probably best to try not to worry about this aspect of things too much and just trust that this side of things will fall into place.

> ## Graduate Perspective
>
> ### Henry Purchase, Civil Engineering graduate
>
> Henry shared his experience at the start of this chapter. We return to him here as he adds to the conversation about one of the best things about his time at university:
>
> *'I loved being able to meet people from all different parts of life and to spark a conversation with them, simply because you had that something in common. However, I did realise after, that it's a bit backwards to pay £40k+ just to meet people – and while I did love meeting all the different people, I often wonder whether I could have had the same enjoyment with less time and financial commitment.*
>
> *'I made two very close friends at uni [though], both of whom I've started businesses with and had many adventures with. When I compare myself to friends who never went to university, the network and friends made during the same period is the big difference.'*

Chapter Recap

▶ University offers more direct opportunities than apprenticeships to expand your social life. Once you're on campus, you will meet people from all kinds of backgrounds who are in the same boat as you, and you will have access to all kinds of clubs and societies.

▶ Apprenticeships don't offer as much social variety but you will still meet other people in the form of work colleagues and other apprentices. In fact, with a little effort, you can make your social life as active as you'd like it to be.

▶ Overall, if expanding your social life and getting more exposure to new people and new experiences is a real priority for you, university could be the stronger option. However, this definitely shouldn't be the only basis for the decision you make, as, ultimately, the power is yours to create the social life you want wherever you are.

Part Three: Conclusion

We've now explored five of the key factors that can guide your decision on what to do after school: scope for career options, your learning preferences, the financial costs, the potential financial rewards, and the kind of social life you would like. Thinking about each of these factors will hopefully have given you insights into what path might be most suitable for you after school – particularly about the university and apprenticeship options, which were the main focus of this section for comparative purposes.

Just to recap on some of the main points: a degree can offer a greater breadth of career choices if you're not sure what you want to do, but is expensive; an apprenticeship is debt-free and allows you to learn skills in a practical way while also earning money, but securing a good training contract is competitive. Both paths can lead to financial security if you work hard; and, while university has social life benefits that are difficult to replicate elsewhere, it wouldn't be ideal to make this the driving factor for any decision.

So it's now time to integrate your thoughts and feelings about these various factors into your overall decision-making process – based on your own personal needs, preferences, desires and goals. In the next section, we'll look at how you can do this through a system that weighs up what matters most to you.

PART FOUR
MAKING YOUR CHOICE

It's now time to pull together all the information we've covered and make a decision about what route seems best for you to pursue after school, with the help of the five key factors that we covered in Part Three. So this section will provide a scoring technique that can guide your ultimate decision, as well as some suggestions on how to deal with deadlock. At the end, I will share my summary thoughts on the initial question posed by this book: 'Is going to uni worth it?'

Note that, for ease of comparison, the scoring process in this section, as in the previous section on the five key factors, will focus on the two most established post-18 education paths of university and apprenticeships. But remember, other routes are also possible, so my hope is that this chapter can serve as inspiration on how to think about any options that interest you.

13
IT'S DECISION TIME

If you've made it this far into the book and already have an idea of what you'd most like to do once you leave school, the scoring exercise in this chapter will hopefully help to reaffirm where you stand. If you're still unsure, it will help to clarify things for you. And if you're stuck somewhere in the middle, we'll look at a few ways you can begin to resolve that feeling of deadlock.

A Few Important Things to Remember

Before we introduce you to the scoring exercise that will help you to identify where you stand in terms of your decision moving forward, it's good to remember some of the key points that Part One highlighted about this process:

1. **There's no such thing as a perfect choice.** Whatever you decide, it will be good in some ways and less good in others. So aim for a 'good enough' choice rather than trying to find the 'perfect' answer (which is unlikely to exist).

2. **This is 'your' choice, not that of your parents, teachers or friends.** It's important to consult your parents, teachers and others who care about you for their insight and guidance. Listen to them and take on board their views, but always keep in mind that this is a choice that *you* have to live through. So, while giving due consideration to the opinions of those closest to you, be sure to give *your* opinion the weight it deserves, rather than being *too* swayed by what *they* think is best for you.

3. **You've made a start, so your future is already looking bright.** Given that you've got this far into this book, you're already off to a good start in terms of the thoughtfulness and commitment that are needed to succeed no matter what path you take in life. If you continue to invest in, and commit to, your development in this way, then I'm confident that you'll have a bright future ahead of you!

How the Scoring Exercise Works

The exercise that follows will help to reveal what your leanings are in terms of whether a university degree or an apprenticeship would be most likely to meet your preferences. Just to be clear, it has not been designed to tell you what to do, as only *you* can make that decision for yourself – including potentially taking an alternative route from the two options under scrutiny here. Instead, it will give you a useful tool to help you make the final decision.

To complete the exercise, you'll need to go through the table on page 189, answering a question for each of the five factors covered

CHAPTER 13 IT'S DECISION TIME

in Part Three – although potentially answering two questions for the first factor (depending on your answer to the first question).

As you answer the question for each factor, you will then be able to assign the appropriate score in the relevant column – either 'University' or 'Apprenticeship'.

Note that each factor has been assigned a 'weighted' score that gives it more or less importance based on the research done for this book. For example, the first factor ('Career Options') has been given a weighting of 35, while the second factor ('Learning Preferences') has been given a weighting of 30. Both factors are important, but if you could only base your decision on one of these factors, you would likely be better off basing it on possible career options rather than whether you can match your learning preferences. This is because learning preferences are something that you can more easily compensate for than career options.

Moving through the rest of the five factors, you will see that 'Financial Costs' has been assigned a weighting of 20, 'Future Financial Rewards' a weighting of 10, and, finally, 'Social Life' a weighting of just 5. In total, the five weighted scores add up to 100.

Be aware that, as you move through the exercise, you can't assign two scores to the same factor. For example, in Career Options, you can't put 35 in the University column *and* 35 in the Apprenticeship column. If you score a factor in one column, you have to place a 0 in the other column.

Once you finish assigning the scores for each factor, complete the subtotal section. The two numbers there should add up to 100.

Sample Exercise Results

Before you try the exercise for yourself, here are a couple of examples of it in action – firstly by a student who ended up leaning towards the university option and, next, by one who ended up leaning towards the apprenticeship route…

University Example

This student has ended up with a total university score of 90 and a total apprenticeship score of 10. It's clear that, from the perspective of this exercise alone, university is therefore likely to be a better fit for this person. Going through each factor we can see the following:

▶ **Career options.** This student isn't sure about what career they want, so likes the idea of having more choices later on. This means they would benefit from a path that provides a broader set of career options, such as those offered by degrees in Maths, Sciences, Engineering, Business/Economics or Languages.

▶ **Learning preferences.** This student enjoys academic learning styles, such as getting to grips with theoretical concepts. They might therefore do well within a university environment.

▶ **Financial costs.** This student understands how student debt works and is comfortable with the concept of repayments in the future. They accept that once they earn more than a certain amount per year, as designated by the UK government, they will make repayments at a set percentage of whatever they make above that figure (see Chapter 10 for a reminder of how this works).

▶ **Future financial rewards.** A high-wage career isn't a priority for this student, which means that either path would

CHAPTER 13 IT'S DECISION TIME

THE FIVE-FACTOR DECISION FRAMEWORK	The Two Major Options	
	University	Apprenticeship
CAREER OPTIONS Do you know what kind of job or career you'd like to do in the future? ☑ No – 35 points to University and skip the next question, going straight to the box below. ☐ Yes – Go to question below Does your ideal job require a degree, or would it benefit from one (for example, investment banking)? ☐ Yes – 35 points to University ☐ No – 35 points to Apprenticeship ☐ Unsure – Research to find out. If you can't find an answer, give 35 points to University.	35	0
LEARNING PREFERENCES Do you prefer academic or practical learning? ☑ Academic – 30 points to University ☐ Practical – 30 points to Apprenticeship	30	0
FINANCIAL COSTS Given what you know now, are you comfortable taking on student debt? ☑ Yes – 20 points to University ☐ No – 20 points to Apprenticeship	20	0
FUTURE FINANCIAL REWARDS Is a high-wage career a major priority? ☐ Yes – 10 points to University ☑ No – 10 points to Apprenticeship	0	10
SOCIAL LIFE Do you wish to boost the number of new people you'll meet? ☑ Yes – 5 points to University ☐ No, or indifferent – 5 points to Apprenticeship	5	0
	SUBTOTAL FOR EACH OPTION	
	90	10
CHECK THAT THE TWO SUBTOTAL COLUMNS ADD UP TO 100	90+10=100	

be fine for them in this regard. There's therefore no point in allocating a score to university here, and the balance can go to the apprenticeship path.

▶ **Social life.** This student is looking forward to an active social life and meeting lots of new people. As such, the score goes to university since that's where it's easier to supercharge your social activities.

Apprentice Example

This student has a total university score of 10 and a total apprenticeship score of 90. This means that, from the perspective of this exercise alone, an apprenticeship is likely to be a better fit for this student than university. Going through each factor we can see the following:

▶ **Career options.** This student knows the career that they would like to pursue and, crucially, has established that jobs in their area of interest don't necessarily need a degree. As various apprenticeship routes are available, university loses its attractiveness with this factor.

▶ **Learning preferences.** This student prefers practical learning and is not keen on writing essays or sitting exams. Because of this, they are likely to do better in an apprenticeship than at uni (although it's important to note that there will be some level of theoretical assessment involved with an apprenticeship as well).

▶ **Financial costs.** This student is not comfortable with the costs of university and the student debt to which this is likely to lead. They would prefer to start earning as soon as possible, rather than spending three years accumulating debt. An apprenticeship path therefore wins for this factor given that it involves no tuition fees.

▶ **Future financial rewards.** This student wants to maximise their chances of earning a high wage. While this can be achieved with an apprenticeship, a strong degree from a top

CHAPTER 13 IT'S DECISION TIME

THE FIVE-FACTOR DECISION FRAMEWORK	The Two Major Options	
	University	Apprenticeship
CAREER OPTIONS Do you know what kind of job or career you'd like to do in the future? ☐ No – 35 points to University and skip the next question, going straight to the box below. ☑ Yes – Go to question below Does your ideal job require a degree, or would it benefit from one (for example, investment banking)? ☐ Yes – 35 points to University ☑ No – 35 points to Apprenticeship ☐ Unsure – Research to find out. If you can't find an answer, give 35 points to University.	0	35
LEARNING PREFERENCES Do you prefer academic or practical learning? ☐ Academic – 30 points to University ☑ Practical – 30 points to Apprenticeship	0	30
FINANCIAL COSTS Given what you know now, are you comfortable taking on student debt? ☐ Yes – 20 points to University ☑ No – 20 points to Apprenticeship	0	20
FUTURE FINANCIAL REWARDS Is a high-wage career a major priority? ☑ Yes – 10 points to University ☐ No – 10 points to Apprenticeship	10	0
SOCIAL LIFE Do you wish to boost the number of new people you'll meet? ☐ Yes – 5 points to University ☑ No, or indifferent – 5 points to Apprenticeship	0	5
	SUBTOTAL FOR EACH OPTION	
	10	90
CHECK THAT THE TWO SUBTOTAL COLUMNS ADD UP TO 100	10+90=100	

university is a more established path to high-wage careers. The score therefore goes to university here.

▶ **Social life.** This student doesn't see the rich and varied social life that's available at university as a priority for them; they are confident in the friendships that they already have and aren't sure university debt is worth it just to grow their social circle. The apprenticeship path therefore gets the points here.

Doing the Exercise for Yourself

Now that you've seen a couple of examples in action, it's time to have a go at completing your own table; you can do this on page 189. Remember: this process is only designed as a *guide* for you, so it does not provide a perfect answer; it simply highlights which way you are leaning with your decision, and why.

Consider Your Result

You should now have a total score for university versus an apprenticeship, and be able to see which path after school you are leaning more towards. What's your gut reaction to this? Is it what you expected? Do you feel excited or a little nervous about what might lie in store for you next? If you're like most people, you'll feel a little anxious either way because this is a decision that matters a lot to you.

Hopefully, you'll now have more helpful information and insight about your choice than you did before. Feel free to talk through your findings with people you trust and respect, as this can help to relieve some of the anxiety you might be feeling over the decision.

CHAPTER 13 IT'S DECISION TIME

THE FIVE-FACTOR DECISION FRAMEWORK	The Two Major Options	
	University	Apprenticeship
CAREER OPTIONS Do you know what kind of job or career you'd like to do in the future? ☐ No – 35 points to University and skip the next question, going straight to the box below. ☐ Yes – Go to question below Does your ideal job require a degree, or would it benefit from one (for example, investment banking)? ☐ Yes – 35 points to University ☐ No – 35 points to Apprenticeship ☐ Unsure – Research to find out. If you can't find an answer, give 35 points to University.		
LEARNING PREFERENCES Do you prefer academic or practical learning? ☐ Academic – 30 points to University ☐ Practical – 30 points to Apprenticeship		
FINANCIAL COSTS Given what you know now, are you comfortable taking on student debt? ☐ Yes – 20 points to University ☐ No – 20 points to Apprenticeship		
FUTURE FINANCIAL REWARDS Is a high-wage career a major priority? ☐ Yes – 10 points to University ☐ No – 10 points to Apprenticeship		
SOCIAL LIFE Do you wish to boost the number of new people you'll meet? ☐ Yes – 5 points to University ☐ No, or indifferent – 5 points to Apprenticeship		
	SUBTOTAL FOR EACH OPTION	
CHECK THAT THE TWO SUBTOTAL COLUMNS ADD UP TO 100		

It's crucial to keep in mind that, although important, this isn't a life-or-death situation. While the choice that you eventually make will lead you in a certain direction on your life's journey, you can always find other routes off a path if you change your mind at any point or don't feel comfortable with the way that things are turning out. We saw a few examples of this earlier in the book, such as Alex Fefegha in the Alternative Perspective box in Chapter 6, for instance.

> **Insight**
>
> **Example of the decision process for someone who aspires to be a pilot**
>
> Opposite is an example of a systematic way in which someone who aspires to be a pilot might analyse their options of what path to take after school – as well as using the scoring exercise on page 189.
>
> In order to be able to compile a comparison list like the one opposite, they would first have to have carried out research into all that is needed to be a pilot and which education and training options would fulfil these requirements; this is what establishes how many 'possible routes' will feature in the chart.
>
> (If you have an idea of what job you might like to do, or what area you might like to work in, it could be really helpful to compile a comparison chart like this for yourself.)
>
> This student might also want to consider an additional factor: the state of the economy in relation to their dream career. For example, as a result of COVID-19, flights were halted globally and many pilots found themselves out of work. For a student making a decision amid these social and economic circumstances, taking time out with a gap year or broadening career options with a degree might therefore be a smarter choice than going to flight school.

CHAPTER 13 IT'S DECISION TIME

If you completed the exercise and got a 50/50 score or somewhere thereabouts, and are still unsure where you stand with your leanings, read the section that follows for more guidance. Otherwise you can head straight to the final 'Summing Up' chapter on page 195.

Possible Routes After School			
Five Factors	**Pilot Training**	**University**	**Apprenticeship**
Career Options	Limited career options after qualification. Specialism is in flying and managing aircraft.	A broad engineering degree would open many doors, and it's possible to consider flight school after graduation.	This is likely to be more specialised, particularly if the course is vocational. However, it's possible to consider flight school after.
Learning Preferences	Practical learning.	Academic learning.	Practical learning.
Costs	Roughly £100,000. This is the most expensive option.	Roughly £50,000. This is the middle option.	Free, with possible annual earnings of £20,000 a year for some Higher Apprenticeships.
Financial Rewards	There's no data on net lifetime earnings, but this is a well-paid career (first officers earn up to £60,000 a year and captains can make £100,000).	£100,000+ extra net lifetime earnings.	£100,000+ extra net lifetime earnings.
Social Life	Limited pilot trainee intake means a less active social life.	Active social life on campus.	Limited apprenticeship intake means less active social life.

How to Deal with Deadlock Scenarios

If you scored 50 for each path, or if the scores were different but close enough that they haven't much helped you with your choice, you can address this 'deadlock' situation by considering a few other possibilities …

Experiments: work experience and university experience days

Whether you're leaning towards one option but are not yet convinced, or you're generally just feeling a little lost or overwhelmed, it can be a great idea to do something that gives you a better taste of your choices without locking you into anything.

For example, if you're thinking about an apprenticeship or going directly into work, you could seek out internships or work experience opportunities over the school holidays – to get a sense of what a certain area of work is like.

Or if you're leaning towards university, you could sign up for an experience day. Many universities offer an opportunity to spend a day or more on campus to see what it's like being a student there. Experiences like this can be really helpful in finding out whether university really is for you.

A third way: Degree Apprenticeships

If you're stuck in the middle of a choice between uni and an apprenticeship, you might like the idea of combining both options. In this instance, a Degree Apprenticeship – as described in Chapter 5 – could be worth looking into.

As discussed in Chapter 5, this option provides the best of both worlds: academic learning *mixed* with substantial practical – and paid – work experience, which allows you to get a degree without student debt (your employer pays for your degree)!

However, as mentioned before, Degree Apprenticeships are often *extremely* competitive. So if you decide to make this route a priority, be sure that you also have a good back-up plan.

Time out: a gap year

Another option explored earlier in the book (this time in Chapter 7) is that of taking a little time out to think things through rather than feeling that you need to make a decision straight away, under pressure. Some students apply for university but defer entry to the following year. Others take a gap year to learn more about themselves so that they can return to the decision-making process with more confidence in the following year (see Chapter 7 for more insight into this).

I hope that these various options help to relieve, at least slightly, any sense of pressure or anxiety that you might be experiencing about what path to take next. Always remember that there's no such thing as a 'perfect choice' here, which means that there's no right or wrong! You just have to take the path that feels instinctively most right for you after you've considered all the factors. And then try to relax into whatever choice you have made in the knowledge that the power lies within *you* to make it the best experience it can be.

14

SUMMING UP: IS GOING TO UNI WORTH IT – FOR *YOU*?

So, back to the question asked in the title of this book: *Is* going to university worth it?

By now you'll have noticed that there's no definitive, 'perfect' or one-size-fits-all answer to this question. The only answer that counts is what will work well for *you*, as an individual.

As we found out way back in Part One of this book, there is no right or wrong path to take. The aim of this book was to equip you with enough knowledge and insight to find an answer that you feel comfortable with, confident about and that works well *enough* for you. This is something that I hope you have now achieved, or that you are at least a lot closer to achieving.

You might, however, still find yourself wondering from time to time, as I have, 'Isn't there a *simpler* answer to the question in hand?' I therefore thought I'd try to sum things up for you – in two different ways. One answer is brief, while the other is a little more involved; but both, essentially, make the same point. So here goes:

Is going to uni worth it? Answer 1: *Yes and no!*
University is worth it for some people, but not for others. Remember, while many people thrive at uni and go on to secure well-paid, satisfying jobs, there are also students who end up financially worse off after university. In fact, some qualified apprentices can earn more than their graduate equivalents and are more satisfied with their choice than degree-holders.

Is going to uni worth it? Answer 2: *It depends on who, what, where and how.*

▶ **The 'who'.** Who's making the decision? *You* are, so what do you want and need? Are you a practical learner or more academic? Do you know what career you want, or are you unsure and would therefore benefit from a path that opens more career options?

▶ **The 'what'.** What do you want to study or train in? For an aspiring doctor, for example, a degree is a must and is definitely worthwhile. But for someone that wants to train as an engineer, carer or social worker, the value of a degree isn't so obvious, especially when apprenticeships of all kinds and levels are available.

▶ **The 'where'.** Where are you thinking of applying? Some elite universities can pay off in ways that an apprenticeship and other universities can't. Many benefit immensely from going to Oxford or Cambridge, for example. However, if you're hard-working and determined, you can still do well without a brand-name university on your CV – or brand-name employer, in the case of apprenticeships.

CHAPTER 14 SUMMING UP: IS GOING TO UNI WORTH IT – FOR YOU?

▶ **The 'how'.** How would you prefer to learn or train? Is hands-on experience in the world of work important to you? Which method of learning will best prepare you for the career you aspire to? How will you fund the university route if it turns out maintenance loans can't cover enough of the living costs?…

All in all then, it should be loud and clear by now that there's no one, simple way to answer the question 'Is going to university worth it?' It should also be evident that university is no longer the obvious 'best choice' in terms of future prospects that many traditionally assume it to be. As such, university should never just be a 'default' choice, since there are so many other potentially rewarding paths out there. Ultimately, it's only *you* who can decide, after careful consideration, which of these paths is the most suitable for *you*. So, whichever one you choose in the end, I wish you much fun, adventure, enrichment and personal fulfilment.

Acknowledgements

Each time I'm at the hardest points of writing a book, those closest to me become all too familiar with the quips I constantly make about how this may be the last book I'll write because of how tricky it can get.

The process of writing is, of course, incredibly rewarding. But it also comes with its fair share of frustrations. And each time I've emerged from these valleys of exasperation with a complete piece of work, I'm reminded of how the finished product would never have been possible without the incredible patience and support of those around me.

For this book in particular – which took far longer to write than I originally planned – Della Oliver was incredibly supportive and more than generous with her patience. I've been fortunate to work with her on all the books I've written so far, and I'm deeply grateful for her guidance over the years.

I'd also like to especially thank Beth Bishop, Kate Michell and Emma Davies at Trotman Publishing. Their feedback and thoughts about the manuscript kept me going and encouraged me to do better. Without this support, the book would not be where it is today.

Finally, I'd like to thank all the fantastic contributors for sharing their experiences with me; my family – and in particular my mother and father, Barbara and Moses Tefula – for inspiring a belief in the power of personal growth through learning; and Laura Gill for cheering me on through the busiest parts of completing this work.

Thank you all for your kindness, love and continued support.

Career essentials
Make your next step with one of our guides

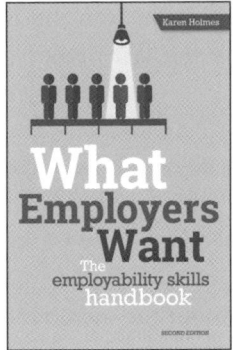

University essentials
Helping you get a head start when applying for university

Helping you get the career you want

For more information and to buy, visit:
www.trotman.co.uk

References

Note: References here list page number, followed by extract from book, followed by source of information.

Preface
ix: *one in four chief executive officers*: www.roberthalf.co.uk/press/route-top-mbas-and-accountants-lead-ftse-100

Introduction
xiii: *tuition fees have had the largest price increase*: www.bankofengland.co.uk/knowledgebank/how-have-prices-changed-over-time

xiii: *lower returns on their investment*: www.hesa.ac.uk/files/Return_to_a_degree_main_report.pdf

Chapter 1: The Art of Making Smart Choices
4: *how the available options relate*: www.youtube.com/watch?v=8GQZuzIdeQQ

5: *'different in kind of value'*: www.youtube.com/watch?v=8GQZuzIdeQQ

8: *in her spare time*: www.ft.com/content/fa5e47c6-0d9b-11e4-815f-00144feabdc0

10: *in her industry*: www.telegraph.co.uk/education/2017/01/12/returning-university-mature-student- changed-career-prospects

14: *'maximisers'*: Schwartz, B., Ward, A., Monterosso, J., Lyubomirsky, S., White, K. and Lehman, D.R., 2002. 'Maximizing versus satisficing: happiness is a matter of choice.' *Journal of Personality and Social Psychology*, 83(5), p.1178

Chapter 2: Learning to Think Independently
22: *a balanced view*: www.suttontrust.com/our-research/apprenticeship-polling-2018

24: *go to university annually*: commonslibrary.parliament.uk/research-briefings/cbp-7857

24: *in the 1960s*: www.lse.ac.uk/assets/richmedia/channels/publicLecturesAndEvents/slides/20131022_1030_ShapingHigherEducationSessionOne_sl.pdf

25: *the economic research group the OECD*: www.oecd.org/unitedkingdom/building-skills-for-all-review-of-england.pdf

25: *graduates in a workplace*: www.theguardian.com/money/2018/sep/11/quarter-of-england-and-n-ireland-graduates-in-school-leaver-jobs

25: *financially worse off*: ifs.org.uk/publications/14729

Chapter 3: Getting to Know Your Underlying Dreams and Aspirations

37: *doesn't make us massively happier*: Aknin, L.B., Norton, M.I. and Dunn, E.W., 2009. 'From wealth to well-being? Money matters, but less than people think.' *The Journal of Positive Psychology*, 4(6), pp.523–527

39: *promote mental wellbeing*: Piliavin, J.A. and Siegl, E., 2007. 'Health benefits of volunteering in the Wisconsin longitudinal study.' *Journal of Health and Social Behavior*, 48(4), pp.450–464

40: *thinking about careers*: www.youtube.com/watch?v=At4kjSXFr-U

Chapter 4: Going to University

45: *apply to go to university:* www.ucas.com/data-and-analysis/undergraduate-statistics-and-reports/ucas-undergraduate-sector-level-end-cycle-data-resources-2020 and commonslibrary.parliament.uk/research-briefings/cbp-7857

45: *course starting in 2021*: www.theguardian.com/education/2021/jul/08/record-set-to-tumble-as-311000-uk-teenagers-apply-for-university

45: *opt to go to university*: commonslibrary.parliament.uk/research-briefings/cbp-7857

45: *who take the apprenticeship path*: explore-education-statistics.service.gov.uk/find-statistics/apprenticeships-and- traineeships/2019-20

45: *by the same age group*: www.ucas.com/data-and-analysis/undergraduate-statistics-and-reports/ucas-undergraduate-end-cycle-reports/2020-end-cycle-report and https://commonslibrary.parliament.uk/research-briefings/sn06113

47: *went to university*: www.suttontrust.com/our-research/elitist-britain-2019

49: *14 hours per week*: www.theuniguide.co.uk/subjects/statistics

49: *teaching per week*: university.which.co.uk/subjects/creative-writing, university.which.co.uk/subjects/law, university.which.co.uk/subjects/business-and-management-studies, university.which.co.uk/subjects/computer-science, university.which.co.uk/subjects/chemistry and university.which.co.uk/subjects/nursing

51: *survey by the Higher Education Policy Institute*: www.hepi.ac.uk/2021/06/24/the-student-academic-experience-survey-2021

52: *to advance their careers*: www.hepi.ac.uk/2020/06/11/the-student-academic-experience-survey-2020

REFERENCES

53: *A 2020 survey by*: www.milkround.com/file/general/MK_CAMPAIGN-Candidate-Compass-2020_Report.pdf

53: *not ready for the workplace*: www.peoplemanagement.co.uk/news/articles/graduates-not-workplace-ready

54: *only 4% were unemployed*: www.hesa.ac.uk/news/18-06-2020/sb257-higher-education-graduate-outcomes-statistics/study

55: *in these types of jobs*: www.hesa.ac.uk/data-and-analysis/publications/destinations-2016-17/introduction

55: *in high-skilled jobs*: explore-education-statistics.service.gov.uk/find-statistics/graduate-labour-markets#dataBlock-e8617dc7-a540-4d56-a726-35cec1a77dda-charts

56: *undergraduates do so*: www.hesa.ac.uk/news/18-06-2020/sb257-higher-education-graduate-outcomes-statistics/study

56: *29% of final-year students*: www.prospects.ac.uk/prospects-press-office/more-than-half-of-final-year-students-lose-jobs

56: *set back their career prospects*: www.ft.com/content/2fc4e1f4-a5e8-4cbd-9bd8-f51a43b01417

Chapter 5: Doing an Apprenticeship

62: *Chichester's first female Member of Parliament*: www.thetimes.co.uk/article/gillian-keegan-from-working-class-merseyside-to-international-business-career-to-tory-mp-s37ncjkjr

62: *compared to six years earlier*: https://explore-education-statistics.service.gov.uk/data-tables/fast-track/f4ed4ab2-ecb3-41f3-88e1-a804a430c416

63: *'good option' for young people*: demosuk.wpengine.com/files/476_1504_CoA_WEB_2_.pdf?1425489134

64: *provide better preparation for life*: www.thetimes.co.uk/article/the-times-view-on-apprenticeships-skills-revolution-0c6c3dkjm

64: *standards are met*: www.legislation.gov.uk/ukpga/2016/12/part/4

65: *National Qualification Level*: www.gov.uk/what-different-qualification-levels-mean/list-of-qualification-levels

66: *vacancies in England alone*: assets.publishing.service.gov.uk/government/uploads/system/uploads/attachment_data/file/962884/apprenticeship_degree_higher_listing_Feb_2021.pdf and explore-education-statistics.service.gov.uk/find-statistics/apprenticeships-and-traineeships/2020-21

68: *170-plus industries*: researchbriefings.files.parliament.uk/documents/SN03052/SN03052.pdf

68: *the National Apprenticeship Service*: www.topapprenticeshipemployers.co.uk/Factsheet_Top100AppEmp20.pdf

72: *for employers and trainers*: assets.publishing.service.gov.uk/

government/uploads/system/uploads/attachment_data/
file/998876/2122_Employer_Rules_Version_Clarification__v1.0.pdf

74: *was £12.46 per hour*: assets.publishing.service.gov.uk/government/
uploads/system/uploads/attachment_data/file/857209/aps-2018-19-gb-
report.pdf

74: *by www.graduate-jobs.com*: www.graduate-jobs.com/gco/Booklet/
graduate-salary-salaries.jsp

74: *struggle to fill roles*: www.bbc.co.uk/news/uk-54341298

74: *an average of £53,200*: www.fmb.org.uk/resource/construction-
apprenticeships-lead-to-a-well-paid-career.html

74: *earners in the UK*: www.gov.uk/government/statistics/percentile-points-
from-1-to-99-for-total-income-before-and-after-tax

75: *for their career plans*: www.gov.uk/government/publications/
apprenticeship-evaluation-2018-to-2019-learner-and-employer-surveys

75: *over half of graduates*: www.pearson.com/content/dam/ global- store/
global/resources/Pearson_Global_Learner_survey_2019.pdf

76: *in work after their training*: www.gov.uk/government/publications/
apprenticeship-evaluation-2018-to-2019-learner-and-employer-surveys

77: *over 9,000 applications*: www.baesystems.com/en/article/bae-systems-
presses-ahead-with-plans-to-recruit-800-apprentices

77: *getting into Oxford*: www.ox.ac.uk/about/facts-and-figures/admissions-
statistics/undergraduate-students

77: *educational charity the Sutton Trust*: www.suttontrust.com/wp-content/
uploads/2020/05/Covid-19-Impacts-Apprenticeships.pdf

Chapter 6: Working Your Way Up

84: *one of the UK's top sports*: Hearn, E., 2020. *Relentless: 12 Rounds to Success*. London: Hodder & Stoughton

Chapter 7: Taking Time Out to Think

95: *whether to go to university or not*: www.thetimes.co.uk/article/here-
come-the-girls-k7qfx3qt998

95: *abandon the university route*: www.thetimes.co.uk/article/cynicism-
and-a-stolen-kiss-with-the-vicars-girl-rfc6xmhvvpw

96: *during their gap year*: www.gov.uk/government/publications/gap-year-
takers-uptake-trends-and-long-term-outcomes

Chapter 8: Your Career Options

109: *require a specific degree*: assets.publishing.service.gov.uk/government/
uploads/system/uploads/attachment_data/file/474254/BIS-15-464-A-
evidence-report-employer-graduate-recruitment.pdf

REFERENCES

109: *don't need a specialist degree:* webarchive.nationalarchives.gov.uk/20180319114826/http://www.hefce.ac.uk/pubs/year/2018/201801 ('Vocational degrees and employment outcomes') and www.gov.uk/government/publications/graduate-choices-in-post-education-jobs-and-careers

112: *related to their studies:* webarchive.nationalarchives.gov.uk/20180319114826/http://www.hefce.ac.uk/pubs/year/2018/201801

Chapter 9: Your Learning Preferences

118: *a food-preference analogy:* 'Stop propagating the learning styles myth.' *Computers & Education*, 106, pp.166–171 and twitter.com/P_A_Kirschner/status/1271516331037384710

123: *the value he got from university*: www.telegraph.co.uk/culture/film/3581259/I-taught-him-now-he-directs-Pacino.html

Chapter 10: The Financial Costs

132: *student debt as the years go on*: www.gov.uk/government/statistics/student-loans-in-england-2020-to-2021

133: *around £9,000 a year*: commonslibrary.parliament.uk/research-briefings/sn00917

133: *for domestic students*: www.gov.uk/student-finance/new-fulltime-students

136: *average weekly accommodation cost*: www.savethestudent.org/accommodation/national-student-accommodation-survey-2021.html

136: *all other expenses*: www.savethestudent.org/money/student-budgeting/what-do-students-spend-their-money-on.html

138: *who started university in 2015*: researchbriefings.files.parliament.uk/documents/SN01079/SN01079.pdf

138: *put this figure at around £5,640*: www.savethestudent.org/student-finance/maintenance-loans.html#amount

138: *might get £3,500*: www.gov.uk/student-finance/new-fulltime-students

140: *one in five students*: ifs.org.uk/uploads/publications/bns/BN217.pdf *and* https://commonslibrary.parliament.uk/student-finance-in-england-how-much-do-graduates-pay-back

141: *to 2020 was 5.6%*: researchbriefings.files.parliament.uk/documents/SN01079/SN01079.pdf

142: *moneysavingexpert.com*: www.moneysavingexpert.com/students/student-loans-tuition-fees-changes

142: *threshold of £27,295 a year*: www.gov.uk/government/news/student-loans-interest-rates-and-repayment-threshold-announcement

143: *support with university costs*: www.savethestudent.org/money/student-money-survey-2020.html

145: *UK parliament briefings in 2021*: https://commonslibrary.parliament.uk/student-finance-in-england-extending-the-loan-term-and-increasing-the-repayment-rates, https://commonslibrary.parliament.uk/student-finance-in-england-impact-of-lowering-the-repayment-threshold and https://commonslibrary.parliament.uk/student-finance-in-england-impact-of-increasing-the-loan-interest-rate

Chapter 11: The Future Financial Rewards

149: *has been on a downward trend*: www.hepi.ac.uk/2021/06/24/the-student-academic-experience-survey-2021

152: *This is the 'net' benefit*: https://assets.publishing.service.gov.uk/government/uploads/system/uploads/attachment_data/file/32419/11-973-returns-to-higher-education-qualifications.pdf

152: *range of £100,000 to £130,000*: ifs.org.uk/publications/14729

153: *£27,400 after five years*: explore-education-statistics.service.gov.uk/find-statistics/graduate-outcomes-leo/2018-19

155: *earnings well below £20,000*: ifs.org.uk/publications/10177

157: *any of the leading institutions*: www.suttontrust.com/wp-content/uploads/2019/12/Elitist-Britain-2019.pdf

157: *high-wage industry by 13%*: Feng, A. and Graetz, G., 2017. 'A question of degree: the effects of degree class on labor market outcomes.' *Economics of Education Review*, 61, pp.140–161

157: *boosted them by 10%*: Feng, A. and Graetz, G., 2017. 'A question of degree: the effects of degree class on labor market outcomes.' *Economics of Education Review*, 61, pp.140–161

158: *rose to 82% in 2020*: www.hesa.ac.uk/data-and-analysis/publications/higher-education-2006-07 and www.hesa.ac.uk/news/27-01-2021/sb258-higher-education-student-statistics/qualifications

161: *up to A level or equivalent*: home.barclays/news/2016/08/apprentices-can-earn-more-than-university-graduates

161: *estimate by the news website MailOnline*: www.dailymail.co.uk/news/article-9876223/How-apprenticeships-leave-young-people-52-732-better-three-years.html

164: *across various institutions*: www.suttontrust.com/wp-content/uploads/2019/12/Levels-of-Success3-1.pdf

Chapter 12: Your Social Life

169: *roughly a third of students*: www.unite-group.co.uk/sites/default/files/2019-09/new-realists-insight-report-2019.pdf